This book belongs to:

Verner
34 Stanley Road
South Orange N. J.
7630547

Letters to a Black Boy

Bob Teague

Letters to

a Black Boy

Walker and Company, New York

First published in the United States of America
in 1968 by Walker and Company, a division of the
Walker Publishing Company, Inc.

Published simultaneously in Canada by The Ryerson
Press, Toronto.

Library of Congress Catalog Card Number: 68-29802

Book designed by Ernst Reichl

Printed in the United States of America

For Adam Fitz-James

You are not the target, my son.
They don't even know you are there.

POSTSCRIPT

In the event of my death, it is my wish that these letters to my son Adam be held for him until he is thirteen years old.

I am not ill, not wanted by the police; the vigilantes are not pounding at my door. But my life is as fragile as the next man's.

I live in a time and place threatened by deliberate or accidental incineration. I am a black man in a society that alternates between denying that I exist and confirming that the quality of my existence shall always be something much less than its laws, its churches and its leading citizens say I have every right to expect. Also, I am all at once a central figure, a pawn, a target and an impotent bystander in the Black Revolution.

Besides those hazards, I deliberately expose my life to other caprices of my time: I drive a car. I breathe polluted air. I smoke a pack of cigarettes every day. Worst of all, I often tell my fellow human beings—including tyrants, madmen and men in power—exactly what I think.

Clearly, the odds against tomorrow are long. It is possible that I may not be around when my infant son has grown up enough to hear some sensible things he ought to know.

B.T.

New York City
May, 1968

Lucidity is the wound nearest to the sun.

—René Char

Dear Adam,

As I begin this letter, Adam, my son, I know exactly what I don't want to say. I don't want to give you advice. What I hope to do is to alert you. My theory is that if you can pick up some idea of what reality is like early, before it intrudes unannounced, you may not be caught off guard—unprepared and undone—as often as most men are.

And there your daddy has an advantage over most men: an eye trained to see things as they are. Not as other men say things are, and not as I would wish things to be. I have developed this eye over seventeen years of gathering and reporting the world's news. News, of course, is nothing more than a daily record of man's stupidities, wisdom, laughter and tears.

In addition to my scholarship in the second oldest profession, I have made the classic mistakes—survived them—and invented a few new ones.

This legacy, then, is your daddy's view of the human landscape.

Perhaps I should begin with something obvious—something so obvious that it escaped my attention for almost thirty-five years: All black men are insane. And that includes your daddy.

Furthermore, it is safe to say that there never has been a sane black man in this society. Almost any living thing would quickly go mad under the unrelenting exposure to the climate created and reserved for black men in a white racist society.

Sometimes I get the feeling that the climate itself is a

1

catalyst, that it reacts with the fluids in a black man's brain to form a bitter, corrosive poison; it eats away the brain cells he needs to develop into a sane representative of humanity.

As a general rule, the white majority has no idea that its irrational behavior has created the monster it calls the Race Problem—better, call it 22,000,000 insane blacks.

I see no reason to apologize for my madness. As a matter of fact, I am proud of it. Any black man who is not insane—the way things are—ought to have his head examined. Our madness is proof of our humanness. As you may recall from history in school, the whites made a big fuss over a relatively little thing, "taxation without representation." They regarded it as an intolerable injustice. And that led them to organize a new country based on fair play and equality. For whites only.

They rarely miss a chance to show a black man that he cannot expect the same.

Just a few months ago, in the spring of 1967, I covered a story that seemed a replay of a bitter moment I had lived with my daddy nearly thirty years earlier. What happened here in New York this year was that an all-white union in the building trades—under pressure from civil rights pickets—gave a written test to your adopted Uncle Julian and several other black men who said they were qualified for membership and the well-paying jobs they couldn't get without the union. All of them passed easily. However, the union decided—that is, some white men decided—that those black men couldn't have gotten those high scores without cheating.

I couldn't say so in my television newscast, but that story brought back vividly the summer of 1937 in Mil-

2

waukee, when I was eight years old. My Aunt Letty, who brought me up, helped my daddy study for a written test for a white union. She knew where to find books on almost anything. Finally, a few days before the test, she said Daddy knew enough to pass. The three of us talked about the things we would buy when my daddy got his union card and began making more money. My dream was a Lone Ranger cowboy suit like the ones I had seen white boys wearing just a few blocks beyond the ghetto.

On the day of the test, however, my daddy returned home sputtering and cursing. "The man said I passed," he told us. "Then the sonofabitch tore up the papers and dropped 'em on the goddamn floor. He claims he seen me cheating. The lying bastard. I never done no such a thing."

My daddy crumpled into a chair at the kitchen table. He hid his eyes and cried. Aunt Letty left the room. I had never seen my daddy cry, and within seconds I was crying, too. He hugged me to his chest and, between his sobs, tried to tell me to hush, that everything would be all right, that he would still buy me that cowboy suit somehow.

My tears had nothing to do with a cowboy suit. I had the feeling—though not the words to explain it—that my daddy would never again be the same. I was crying for what had been stolen from him, and for the hurt I knew he would feel for the rest of his tomorrows.

What they stole from my daddy they later stole from me when I became a man, a little piece at a time. In self-defense—trying to hang on to what I thought was the real me—I replaced the stolen pieces with bitterness, suspicion and rage. These are not satisfactory substitutes. They cannot help me to become the person I might have been. They

3

serve mainly to keep me on guard against further losses to the enemy. Which means that there is still enough of the real me left to reject their notion of what I am, what I can do, what I deserve and where they think I belong. In other words, I am at odds with the main theme of this society. And I still dream of the man I could have been if they had let me alone.

Now that you know that your daddy is a madman and why, I think you may understand my satisfaction in telling you this: My recognition of my madness has been a great strength and comfort. Instead of just plain crazy, it has made me crazy like a fox. It has released me from some of the subtle tyrannies that can combine with the less subtle to accelerate a black's insanity until he is a shell of a man.

How much of a man could I be in my own eyes if I accepted Mister Charlie's notions? One of his favorite subtle tyrannies goes like this: "Sure, we know the blacks should be equal, but they just aren't ready yet."

By the clear light of my madness I can see that Mister Charlie has raised a lie into a principle. According to the basic law of white American society—of humanity—equality is the natural condition of man. No one has to pass a test. And no man—white, black or polka dot—is given any right to appoint himself judge of another man's "readiness."

Another of Mister Charlie's subtle tyrannies—designed to keep things as they are—goes like this: "Why don't the blacks pull themselves up by their bootstraps? You know, like the Irish, the Jews and the other minorities did."

But Mister Charlie is extremely reluctant to let a black man get a pair of boots. He has not treated all minorities alike, simply because the other minorities have not been

4

so visible as targets. They looked like Mister Charlie himself. So much so that many of them have joined his conspiracy against blacks.

It is equally difficult for Mister Charlie to hear the false note in his harpings on ungratefulness. "You complain about not having a decent place to live," he says. "So we build you a whole new neighborhood of decent places. With low rents, to boot. But what happens? You break the windows, piss in the hallways, and practically tear it down overnight."

In his scorn, he never listens when you try to explain that moving black folk from an old ghetto into a new ghetto is not facing the problem. That opening a low-income housing project for Negroes still leaves you locked out from the kind of jobs, dignity and advanced education that would one day enable you to get something better through your own sweat. That it is therefore impossible to take pride in any charity while still struggling against a system that prevents you from rising to a level where you can develop pride in yourself.

The remarkable thing about Mister Charlie is that he believes his own lies. And that, of course, means it would be futile and stupid of black men to expect Mister Charlie to effect changes that mean anything. He moves only as far and only as fast as fear forces him. Somewhere deep in his bones he knows that if he were placed in such a ridiculous position he would fight.

Great guns in the ghettos! Must it always come down to that?

Well, your daddy has given that question a great deal of thought, and my answer is different from Mister Charlie's. I know deep in my bones that there is only one way

5

to put things right in this society. The question is whether Mister Charlie is man enough to face it.

But we'll have to get to that later because

> *If a boy is to calculate*
> *The weight of 2 plus 2*
> *He first must grasp*
> *What numbers are*
> *And why a sum is due.*

Dear Adam,

Great puddles in the playpen! What a fabulous infant you are.

All at once this week in a sudden burst of creativity you accomplished two miracles, my son. You learned to say four words quite clearly: *football*, *daddy* and *Tall Lady*, a nickname your mother may never lose.

Your second miracle was even more astonishing to your daddy: You stood up and walked like a man.

The manner in which you mastered these feats—trial and error—is worth remembering, my son. It may help you later with the complicated problems outlined in these letters. After all, separating what is from what isn't, and exchanging myths and superstitions for more reliable guides is like learning to walk and talk. You have to test first one method and then another.

Dear Adam,

Early this evening, my son—just before the Tall Lady coaxed you into leaving your puzzle blocks, and bundled you off to bed—you tottered into my study at a moment that struck me as symbolic.

This is my day off from broadcasting the news, and I was watching a television newscast as you came lurching through the doorway, eager and expectant. On the screen at that moment was a black man, angry and proud, being led to jail by white policemen. His name is H. Rap Brown —by now, as you read this, probably a legend if not a martyr.

I have never met H. Rap Brown; but this evening, as I watched him being led to jail, I recognized him as the secret black man inside my own black skin who has been trying all these years to get out.

H. Rap Brown stands taller than most black men I have ever seen; that is, he allows absolutely no injustice by hunkies to go unchallenged. As I watched him on the screen, I thought: How much closer might black men be to freedom now if all of us had faced all of them with Rap Brown's kind of courage?

And there at my feet was a black boy growing up in an age being shaped in no small measure by H. Rap Brown and a thousand angry men just like him. As these go, let others come.

I picked you up from the floor, and we played your favorite bouncing game, with you astride my knees. You laughed. I laughed, too. But I was thinking of other things.

When Adam is as old as Rap Brown, I wondered, how much or how little like Brown will he be? Will he reject me, his daddy, as useless and obsolete? Very probably, I supposed. After all, I am not like Rap Brown except in spirit. I am not in the front lines. At best, I am a distant soul brother, enjoying the comforts of the relatively uninvolved middle class while reaping the benefits of his Black Revolution.

It is entirely possible, I thought, that Adam may be ashamed.

Although I felt a sense of loss as I asked these questions and guessed the answers, I tried at the same time to be realistic. I reminded myself that there is always a gap, if not a gulf, between the generations of a father and his son. The gap between my father and me had been so great that I left home at seventeen. It was many years before I began to understand my daddy even a little. And since then, I have done my best to make amends.

What I hadn't understood as a teen-ager was that my daddy had grown up in a very different world. In his growing-up time, the early 1900's, there was no such thing as a Negro protest movement, no such animal as H. Rap Brown. And in those days the phrase *civil rights* had nothing to do with black men.

To me as a teen-ager, my daddy was a shameless clown. He was overanxious to please Mister Charlie, regardless of personal indignities. What annoyed me most in my early know-it-all years was the beaten, apologetic look always in his eyes. "If you don't kick me too hard," his soft brown eyes seemed to say, "I'll try not to cry too loud."

9

My daddy was not alone, of course. That look of utter defeat and surrender could be called the trademark of his generation. As a teen-ager, I saw it in the eyes of nearly all black adults.

What about my generation? Well, as I look back on my young adult years in the 1950's, I remember a spark of pride and confidence in the eyes of black men around my age. To me, the message in their eyes was: "I know I can, and I will."

I believe it was in my eyes, too. Partly because the world had changed in a small but important way. Mister Charlie was a trifle shaky about the righteousness of racism, after having fought a war against Nazi Germany, the most determined racists of the century.

A major change for me and my generation was exposure to some of what hunky children had been getting all along. In other words, Mister Charlie opened a few doors. My generation surged through, prodded by the dreams of those defeated black men and women we called momma and daddy.

I remember being less than enthusiastic about school. I was fond of playing hooky. My daddy cured me by giving my hide an extra tanning, and terse lectures: "I don't want my boy to have to take what I've had to take from the white man all my life. And if you don't stay in school, you'll wind up just like me—getting nothing but the white man's leavings."

Now, many years after those lecture-demonstrations, I sense that there will probably be a distance between you, my son, and me. We seem to be twice removed already because there is another generation between us—H. Rap Brown's generation of black men marching, shouting, fighting, burning and demanding freedom now. Theirs, yours and mine. When I look into *their* eyes, I see: "This is as far as we go under the hunkies' rules. From here on out, it's war."

Your generation will be unlike mine, which learned only gradually that black men should always protest injustice. Your generation—following Rap Brown's—is likely to grow up taking it for granted that black men should always fight back.

Even as out-of-date as my generation will seem to you, we—I—want what Rap Brown's generation wants. I want it even more for you. It goes without saying that you will want it, too. Exactly how you go about getting it is something I may not even be able to envision here on a warm spring night in 1967. But this you should know:

Each man has to fight for what he believes in, for what he wants, in his own terms.

If Rap Brown's way fits you, then so be it. If you would rather join your will to economic boycotts or civil disobedience, so be it. If you would prefer to work with whites for change through the negotiation process they prefer, so be it. If you would rather concentrate on one aspect of the problem, such as teaching or counseling less fortunate blacks in the ghettos, so be it. And if you don't want to do anything but live your own life, so be it.

But whatever you do, let it be your decision, growing from your convictions—not Rap Brown's, not mine or anyone else's. Let no man sell you his battle cry.

It is your life, my son. And the moments that mean most in it will be those when you do what you feel you must. Because of an urgent command from your guts.

Dear Adam,

For dinner tonight, the Tall Lady served corn bread, black-eyed peas and chitterlings—better known as chit'lins. You know by now as you read this—because we will have taught you—that those dishes are staples in almost any black household that has abandoned the old-fashioned game that might be called Our Skins Are Black but We Are Not Typical Negroes. One of the many black comedies you will not have to perform.

There was a time, not many years ago, when such self-humiliation was in vogue.

When your daddy and the Tall Lady became husband and wife, in 1955, we were typical refugees from the ghetto. We had fled—physically and mentally—into what we thought was middle-class respectability. Out of shame, we avoided "soul food" like tonight's dinner and all other symbols of our past. We saw ourselves as the new Negroes. The ones who would prove to white society that all black folk aren't as primitive and stupid as Stepin Fetchit—one of the few black men we saw in the movies when we were growing up. Our deliberate denials of ourselves amounted to self-hypnosis. We actually believed that we were different. Our prejudice was against Negroes below the middle class—those who were not college graduates and who almost always lived in the ghetto, as best they could, on less than $5,000 a year. That covered most black people in this country. We felt embarrassed in public when we met a Negro who was poor, dirty, drunk, disorderly—Mister Charlie's image of black men. That kind, we thought, just make it harder for the rest of us. Like Mister Charlie, we

12

insisted irrationally that those unfortunate Negroes should conduct themselves at all times like respectable middle-class white folk. Then, we reasoned along with Mister Charlie, things would get better for all of us.

Both the Tall Lady and I are appalled now, a dozen years later, that we ever played that terrible, stupid game.

In 1957, there entered into our insulated lives a proud black man who called himself Minister Malcolm X. And through him, we began the long journey back—back to the Negro race and back to ourselves.

"The white man is the devil," Malcolm X shouted with anger and conviction. "He's the real cause of all our problems in this country."

Minister Malcolm was speaking at a sidewalk rally at 125th Street and Seventh Avenue in the heart of Harlem. *The New York Times* news department had borrowed me from the sports beat to get the inside story on this new and apparently dangerous voice in the ghetto. His was a voice that preached what *The Times* people called "black nationalism." I had never heard of it at all.

I took the Tall Lady with me on this assignment in Harlem, in the spirit of what the white magazines we used to read called "togetherness."

Anyway, we were shocked. We had never heard a black man shout his condemnation of the white man in public. I can remember glancing over my shoulder, half expecting to see white vigilantes moving in to take him away. I saw a few white reporters and white policemen bordering the solid black crowd that was applauding Malcolm X. But none of the whites said a word or made a move. From the looks in their faces, though, they were as uncomfortable as the Tall Lady and I. For quite different reasons.

Because I was a reporter from *The Times*—the most

respected newspaper in Christendom—and because my skin was black, I was able to get an exclusive interview with Malcolm X a few days later. Once again I took the Tall Lady with me. This time, however, I was proving to Malcolm X and his Black Muslims that even though I was making it in the white world, I was not one of those turncoat Negroes who tried to deny their blackness further by marrying white.

Even so, Minister Malcolm was suspicious of me. With some justification. We were sitting at a table in the Crescent Cafe, a restaurant in Harlem owned and operated by the Muslims. Fixing me with accusing, penetrating eyes, he said: "They sent you up here to be a stool pigeon, didn't they?"

And before I could frame a denial that would not sound like a lie, he added: "You poor, poor fool."

Malcolm X knew a lost soul brother when he saw one.

Patiently, almost paternally, he explained what black nationalism was all about: Demanding justice in the white man's world instead of begging for it; fighting back instead of turning the other cheek; calling attention to the fact that the white man could not be trusted except in very special situations; protecting your wife and children from the violence and indignities so casually meted out by white society; and being proud of your race instead of trying to deny your membership in it.

Minister Malcolm was cool, intelligent, articulate. Quietly, he told us what Mister Charlie had done to us and would one day do to our children yet unborn. He was the first black madman we had met who had looked his madness in the eye. His detailed analysis of Mister Charlie's deep commitment to white supremacy was so compelling that no thinking black mind could deny it.

14

That was the beginning of our awareness of our madness, the Tall Lady's and mine. Malcolm X had helped us to break through the flimsy façade we had constructed. And all of a sudden, to our great surprise, we could relax. We could stop pretending. We could be ourselves.

It was wonderful.

Dear Adam,

Question the mysteries that you
do not understand
Question the answers that
quickly come to hand
Question your teachers, yourself
and what you see
Question him, question her
Question me

Despite your daddy's desire simply to guide you through the maze, there will be times when I am guilty of pushing and preaching. My excuse is that I cannot forget that the black skin you got from me will force you to waste a king-size slice of your lifetime climbing invisible barriers, imagining other barriers where none exist, fending off affronts—real and imagined—to your dignity, proving that you are human, disproving that you are inferior, living down stereotypes, protesting injustice, choking down helpless rage, waiting for freedom, and adjusting to the knowledge that you will still be waiting when you die.

All those distractions, of course, will rob you of more time and energy than any man can afford to lose from his search for personal fulfillment, from learning to help, to share, to build, to laugh, to dream, to love.

And that is why with a sense of desperation I pound away, trying to instill in you the notion that the real concerns of living have no relation to the color of your skin; that besides learning to cope with the distractions that come

16

with being black in this society, you must also face the more fundamental distractions that plague all men.

I am confident that you will learn to handle both kinds —also that you will not be harmed by my pushing and preaching—if you can maintain and apply the same innocent skepticism you have brought to each fresh puzzlement you have faced beyond the womb.

My ego whispers in gloating tones that this innocent skepticism was a gift from me to you through my seed. I can't tell you exactly how I got it, but I can remember when I recognized it, and what led me to make it an article of faith.

It was the last week of August in my seventeenth summer, the beginning of my senior year in high school. I went to old Doc Gilmer in his second-floor office over the 711 Bar on Walnut Street, the main street in my ghetto.

"We start football practice next week, Doc," I said, placing a printed yellow card on his desk. "I need an okay from you, same as last year, to let them know I'm still healthy enough to play."

Old Doc Gilmer had been poking in my ears, looking over his spectacles at my tongue and thumping my chest for almost as many years as I could remember. He had never found anything beyond the usual childhood ailments. Still, his strong brown fingers, gnarled by arthritis, poked and probed as thoughtfully as if I were some stranger. It was a routine examination until old Doc Gilmer placed the business end of his stethoscope over my heart. He listened. He frowned. He glanced at me over his spectacles. He readjusted the listening tubes in his ears, then frowned some more.

17

"Young man," he said finally, removing the stethoscope from my chest, "your football days are over."

I could feel my eyes widen. But I was too stunned to protest. I dreaded his next words.

"In fact," he continued slowly, "you really ought to be at home lying down right now. Your heart valves have gone bad. You're going to have to take things very, very easy . . . avoid strenuous activity and overexcitement."

By that time my heart was bumping the back of my throat. I tried by an act of will to slow it down, to hold back what I now thought of as a ruined thing wearing itself out too soon for no reason.

"Am I going to die, Doc?" I finally croaked at him.

He smiled, but only faintly. "Oh, no. Nothing like that. Not if you remember to be careful."

In the silence that fell, there was only the sound of his fountain pen scratching the verdict on my yellow card. And that relentless pounding in my ears.

I left the doctor's office in shock. My eyes saw nothing of my surroundings, focused instead on the vision of my new future: A quiet life without the joys and furies I had grown to love and need, a life of measured pleasures between polite apologies and refusals. For me, going on seventeen, no life at all. If self-pity could destroy, I would have drowned in its wave.

Hours passed before I was able to manage anything that resembled thinking. I suddenly realized, at dusk, that I had wandered miles from my neighborhood. I could have been having a bad dream, I hoped. But no. That terrible yellow card was still in my pocket with its uncompromising verdict: "This boy's heart is not strong enough for competitive athletics."

18

I tried to imagine what school would be like without football, what I would be like as a walking invalid. I saw myself tiptoeing around on eggshells, waiting for the day when some unexpected challenge would burst my heart.

And all at once my mind was clear. I was calm and quiet inside. I decided not to tell anyone my secret, and pray that Doc Gilmer might never get around to telephoning my home to see if I was following orders.

I went into the nearest drugstore and spent thirty-nine cents on a bottle of ink remover. That night, alone in my room, I carefully revised my death warrant. I scrawled a forgery of old Doc Gilmer's handwriting: "Splendid physical specimen—approved for all athletics."

In my own mind, it was still a death warrant, but I could live with it. I would die living. Not cringing.

Through almost every moment of every practice session and through the first two football games of the season, I half expected each play from scrimmage to be my last. But nothing happened. Gradually, I began to doubt old Doc Gilmer's diagnosis. Strangely, it had never previously crossed my mind to question his findings. After all, he was the doctor. Why would he tell me anything less than the truth?

Doctor Howard was a much younger man than old Doc Gilmer, and perhaps a better doctor. But the main reason I went to his office, in mid-season, was that he was new in town, a stranger. I gave him a phony name. He poked, thumped and listened to my heart, then gave me the best news I ever heard: "Young fella, you're probably the best physical specimen I've ever examined."

I never went back to old Doc Gilmer to tell him of his mistake. But since then I have spared my nervous system a great deal of wear and tear, and avoided countless mistakes by approaching most situations as if they were checkups in old Doc Gilmer's office.

So again, as I said, no harm will come of my pushing and preaching if you carry the seed of my doubt.

Dear Adam,

While whispering our conceits about you tonight, my son, hovering over the crib as you slept, we felt a familiar mixture of sadness and rage. The Tall Lady summed it up:

"Isn't it a crime that they'll try to push Adam into a corner without trying to see what kind of human being he happens to be? He's a beautiful boy with a lot of kindness and intelligence. But that's something the Mister Charlies of this world will ignore."

Great hunkies on the hilltops! How many black mothers have said that?

Your daddy was reminded of something that I've had to tell myself almost every day while running an endless gantlet: The hunkies have nothing against you personally, I tell myself over and over again. Though they insult you or ignore you, it has nothing to do with anything you are or might have done. They are responding to the color of your skin and a myth about blackness stamped upon their brains. But that's *their* hang-up, their special madness. So relax. Don't let their taunts and snubs get you down.

You are not the target, my son. They don't even know you are there.

Dear Adam,

I was a bit miffed today by your response to me when the Tall Lady went shopping and left us alone. No matter what games I devised, you made it clear that you would not be satisfied till she returned.

Every five minutes, it seemed, you would break off whatever we were doing and crawl to the front door. "Taw Lady? Taw Lady?" was the only question you could phrase. You would remain at the door—a questioning look on your face—until I opened it to prove that she was not just beyond it in the hallway. I also tried to explain that she had gone to the supermarket. But you had no idea of what your daddy was driving at. We must have repeated that routine a dozen times.

Anyway, new fathers are sensitive about things like that. It makes them feel useless.

Not that I don't fully understand your point of view. Daddies are seldom there when you need them. They seem to be always off fixing, building, changing or destroying some part of the outside world. Mothers, on the other hand, are dependable. Furthermore, they have patience for the hundred tiny details so important to your sense of well-being. I felt exactly the same about the only mother I ever knew, Aunt Letty.

When my real mother died giving birth to me, Aunt Letty, her sister, dropped whatever she was doing in Detroit, and came to live with me and my daddy in Milwaukee. I never did find out what it was she left behind. Her reasoning, I gathered years later, was that to know

22

might have given me a feeling of guilt. Or of being in her debt.

Whatever it was, Aunt Letty seemed to have no regrets. She plunged into the job of helping a squalling black infant to grow up. She stayed with us until I went away to college at seventeen.

By then she had taught me what I still regard as the most important lesson a black boy has to learn. She convinced me that life was much larger than the limits imposed on us for the color of our skins; that I must keep in mind that my world is bigger than the boundaries of the ghetto, that it is a world of different pains and pleasures, beauty and ugliness, victories and defeats that all men everywhere come to know. She taught me to dream beyond my blackness.

Years later, she taught the entire family how to make a common dream come true.

During the Thanksgiving Day recess of my sophomore year in college, she invited—no, she ordered—the whole clan to dinner. By then, she had won her master's degree and was teaching at a small teachers college. My daddy and I drove three hundred miles in his 1937 Chevrolet to see the old girl in Detroit.

When we arrived at Aunt Letty's four-room apartment on Twelfth Street in the ghetto, the others were already there. I met fourteen strangers—relatives I had never seen before. But I felt our kinship immediately. Three of the men and two of the women—my daddy's brothers and sisters—reminded me of him. There was also something in their features—eyes, noses and chins—that looked like me. Two other women—my mother's sisters—who were standing next to their husbands, showed a resemblance to the

23

pictures of her my daddy kept. Aunt Kathleen and Aunt Thelma. My daddy's sisters were Aunt Sally and Aunt Minnie, both with husbands. My daddy's brothers, with their wives, were Uncle Mark, Uncle James and Uncle Claybourn Junior. Although all of them had children, I was the only nonadult present. Aunt Letty had told the others to leave their kids at home; that this was to be an important meeting. I was flattered that she regarded me, at eighteen, as a man.

Aunt Letty had stuffed three turkeys for the occasion, but her dining room was not big enough for the herd she had invited. We served ourselves from the table, then filled the chairs, the stools and the couch in the living room. Some of us wound up sitting on the floor.

During the meal, there was much reminiscing among my daddy and his brothers, who had not seen one another for nearly twenty years. I gathered from their talk that their daddy—my grandfather Claybourn—had been a tough old codger when they were boys together in Tennessee. Almost every story ended with "and then Poppa Claybourn whupped me till I couldn't sit down." Laughter. I was glad that my daddy remembered those "whuppings." It explained why he had spanked me less than a dozen times when I was a boy. As a rule, he had punished me instead by denying privileges. Such as Western movies on Saturday mornings at the Princess Theater.

Finally, when we began eating dessert—sweet potato pie —Aunt Letty made a little speech.

"This is the first time we've been together as a family, but I hope it won't be the last. The thing that prompted me to call you all together was a letter I received a few months ago from James there. He wanted to know if there

24

was anything I could do to help his boy Raymond get to college. In case you haven't heard, Raymond wants to be an airline pilot."

She paused as some of her sisters and brothers-in-law caught their breaths and groaned sympathetically.

"I know what you're thinking," Aunt Letty went on. "It's a terribly big dream for a black boy to have in Tennessee. But I say why not? I say Raymond ought to have his chance to follow his dream. I say that's what living is all about. I say chances are that boy will wind up in a foundry just like his father unless he gets that chance. And I say all the children in this family—the girls, too —should have their chance. Now none of us at the moment can afford to send anybody to college. It's terribly expensive. But if we stick together as a family, we can send them all, one or two at a time. Confucius say, 'What one man find impossible, seventeen men and women find simple.' "

Aunt Letty is fond of crediting the most unlikely wisdom to Confucius.

She went on to explain her idea of a fund that each branch of the family would contribute to every year—an assistance plan that even Confucius might have called a *hui*—to guarantee college for every child who dreamed of going. She didn't bother asking for a vote. She could tell from the looks on our faces—and from the tears in the women's eyes—that she was providing the answer to many prayers.

Dear Son,

Although at the age of one you are much too young to be faced with the horrors of discipline, you are getting your first lessons this week. Just the barest unavoidable minimum—nothing like the maze of do's and don't's that lie ahead.

The Tall Lady and I agreed a few days ago, after seeing you gulp down a button, that you have to learn the correct response to "No." You have become so strong, so active, so curious, destructive and unpredictable that we have nicknamed you the Adam-Smasher.

Even when you are thirteen years old, you will scarcely be able to imagine what the Tall Lady and your daddy felt inside as nearly all the first fifty "no's" made you cry. And the look in those innocent eyes as they brim and glisten with tears. The message is painfully clear: "I've been betrayed."

To keep saying no, we have to remind ourselves that, innocent as you may appear, you are still the Adam-Smasher. Our greatest fear is that you may wind up smashing Adam.

Now that you are older, as you read this—thirteen years instead of one year—you are learning that the frustrations of rules and restrictions are endless.

When your daddy was a boy, it seemed to me that as I grew bigger, so did the world. The rules and frustrations multiplied in number, kind and complexity.

But gradually it all became at least bearable; and in some instances, comforting—like having a map in a wilder-

26

ness. And most of all, my acceptance of the rules became easier as I began to grasp why they existed in the first place —to give a shape to life and protect it.

Much later, I stumbled upon this classic explanation in a book: "The covenant by which man creates a community is an agreement to forego the perilous gratifications of animal existence for the more permanent advantages of human fellowship; and the law is a detailed statement of that covenant."

As all men discover soon or late, however, I found that some of the rules go too far—that it is one thing to soften the rough edges inside a man, but quite another to deprive him of the essence of manhood.

The penalties for breaking such rules are often very great, sometimes excessive. On occasion, though, your daddy has ignored them. And I still do. I deeply believe that each man owes it to himself and to his son to reject the stupidities of his time. Otherwise, the world would never change for the better.

Dear Adam,

Well, you finally did it, Adam-Smasher.

Despite warnings, threats and advice, you removed the plastic safety plug from a wall socket in the dining room and jammed a small key into the outlet. Judging from the Tall Lady's hysterical recap of your adventure when I got home this evening, you came *that* close to being electrocuted.

I don't mind admitting that I was slightly hysterical myself for about thirty seconds. The Tall Lady managed to interrupt my ravings about her failure to "protect that boy from himself."

"He wasn't hurt," she shouted back. "Not even a scratch!" Then, in a quieter tone, she added: "He must have let go of the key the instant he plugged it in. I was in the kitchen when it happened, and I came out running right away, almost knowing what had happened. I had heard sort of a popping noise, and the radio went dead. Adam was standing by the wall socket, which was scorched black. The key had sort of melted in the outlet. His hand —his left hand—was covered with the same black stuff just like the socket. I thought he might have burned his fingers something terrible. But he wasn't crying. At least he wasn't until I started crying when I saw those scorched-looking fingers. It turned out, though, that he wasn't burned at all. The black stuff came off completely when I washed his hand."

Well.

Although your daddy felt much better after that, he

still required first aid. "Darling," I said, "I'd like a double martini if you please. And don't fool around with that vermouth."

Halfway through that soothing dose of medicine, I was feeling pleased that you had tested the socket with that key. In the first place, you had used your left hand, the Tall Lady said. Which meant that you're probably going to be a southpaw just like me. It's a small point, I know. But small points count very big with daddies as they strain to see themselves in their sons.

I had another reason for being pleased. It was not so much that you had survived. I took that for granted by now. What impressed me was the subtle evidence that you were going to be one of the lucky ones. Luck also counts very big in your daddy's views of things. I have faith—call it superstition if you will—in my luck. I say any boy— black, white or chartreuse—needs luck just to survive on this planet. And to avoid being too badly scarred, mentally, by the disappointments and heartaches all of us meet while here.

Judging from this evidence, I was even encouraged to believe tonight that your spirit will escape uncrippled from your first real jolt of bigotry. But it will be a jolt. It always is, no matter how much warning a black boy may have had.

Mine came at the age of six and a half. While I flatter myself that I was able to recover in a sawed-off jiffy, the experience is still vivid thirty-two years later.

In those days—the early 1930's—I lived on Veliet Street in Milwaukee with my daddy and Aunt Letty. To me Aunt Letty was always a teacher, even before she was licensed for schools. She taught me singing to help me drop the lazy speech habits all black boys develop in the ghettos. My speech was much like my daddy's, and much like that of the other daddies in my neighborhood. All of those daddies had grown up in the South. Most of them were grammar-school dropouts.

According to Aunt Letty, I would never amount to anything unless my speech improved. "Confucius say," she improvised, "boy who speak like hobo soon grow from boy to tramp."

Anyway, thanks to Confucius and Aunt Letty, I became an excellent singer. At least that's what everyone in my neighborhood and my Sunday school class said.

Then the news came to my block that the Clarion Theater—the most elegant movie house on the white fringe of the ghetto—planned an amateur contest on its stage in connection with the latest Shirley Temple movie. First prize would be five hundred dollars in cash and a trip to Hollywood for a screen test.

All my friends urged me to enter the contest, saying I might wind up being a black boy Shirley Temple.

Me? In the movies? Singing and dancing like Shirley Temple? Wow! It was the kind of dream that would keep any child awake through the night. Shirley Temple was a chubby bundle of talent with dimples and long blond curls —the undisputed goddess of a nation that worshiped children. She was a millionaire before she had reached her teens.

To my friends I pretended indifference. I said nothing about it to Aunt Letty or my daddy. But secretly, I practiced my favorite song—the one that begins, "I think that I shall never see a poem lovely as a tree." And a few days later, with the contest only a week away, I sneaked off to enter.

30

There was a tall white usher in a dashing blue uniform —gold braid and brass buttons—standing under the Clarion Theater marquee. When I asked him where I should go to put my name in for the contest, he said gruffly: "Go home, boy. It's for whites only."

I had been warned that there were places and things in the world strictly out of bounds for Negroes. But I had never faced any of them, personally, all alone. The shock was indescribable. I turned and ran as fast as my legs would carry me.

I was spurred by an overpowering jumble of emotions, which I identified years later as shame, frustration and rage. As I ran toward the safety of home, bawling and weeping through the streets, I remember thinking that I could have accepted losing the contest. Or even not being allowed to compete. If only they had waited to make up their minds until after I had a chance to sing "Trees."

Dear Adam,

The Tall Lady was looking over my shoulder earlier to-night as I was writing another letter to you. "You've left out at least three important things that Adam should know," she said. I didn't waste time asking what she had in mind, knowing that she would tell me anyway.

"You haven't told him," she went on, "that Mister Charlie wouldn't recognize a black man as an individual person even if they met on the moon. You haven't said that it's important to keep your sense of humor in spite of it all. And you haven't told him that with a sense of humor you can survive."

I had to admit she was right.

"Why don't you tell him about the time we went to the Virgin Islands?" she said. "I'll never forget the look on your face."

I remembered then. But it was more her story than mine, I decided, and asked her to tell it to you. She sat down at my place, and two hours later she handed me a rather romantic version of the incident, which she entitled:

THE WHITE DINNER JACKET

She loved the way her husband looked: Tall, athleti-cally lean body and coconut-shell brown skin with a sheen that made her think of ripe plums. When it came to her husband, she was always romantic, and kept a constant secret game going. As she watched him approach some street corner where they had agreed to meet,

32

she would imagine away the sidewalk and substitute a white sand beach, shed his city suit, dress him in a batik loincloth, and sling a bright-colored tropical bird across his shoulder. The hunter home from the hill.

He would stroll toward her with his natural islander's gait, and it was an African prince, or the original Adam himself, she went to meet.

Eventually, though, when they began planning their Caribbean vacation, she gave up the games of Adam and Eve and African prince. She started the dinner-jacket game. Whenever she came across a travel folder or a cigarette ad—set casually but formally aboard ship or in a palm-roofed dining pavilion—she would substitute her husband for all the lifeless, orange-skinned manikins. He would be twice as handsome; infinitely more dazzling with his coconut-shell color and plum-skin sheen.

Prompted by her game-dream, she asked her husband: "Why don't you buy a dinner jacket, honey? You'd look so beautiful in one."

"Yes, well it's not essential in the islands; but perhaps on a lunch hour I'll pick one up." Although he answered promptly, she could tell by his tone that he was dismissing the subject entirely. She was not disheartened, however.

As they were packing their bags on the night before they left for vacation—no dinner jacket had appeared—she said casually: "Well, you forgot to buy the dinner jacket; but that's all right. We'll buy one when we get there."

His only response was a grunt.

Away from his office and the job, possessed by a holi-

33

day spirit of anything goes, he relaxed under the shimmering blue skies and the ever-present tropical sun that warmed the islands. It was no problem at all to guide him into the hotel haberdashery the same day they arrived. Shopping with rum punch in hand, amid seashell and fishnet décor, with the ocean just across the street, was not at all like the tug of wars she had known in New York City, at Macy's, Bloomingdale's and Gimbel's.

He tried on jacket after jacket. She, eyes bright with excitement and pride, finally selected the one she liked best—a smooth but loosely fitting white one. The lapels framed his throat and face elegantly. And the madras cummerbund added a jaunty native touch. The coat rested on his shoulders, then swung down gracefully, ending below the hips, giving no definition of the body beneath.

As he posed in front of the bamboo-framed mirror, he glanced indifferently at his reflection, but basked in her approval. Then a stray breeze caught inside the jacket, causing it to bell out—causing her to think of a sail made convex by the wind and shielding a sailor in its curve. Feeling the gentle breeze and looking through the door of the shop toward the blue-green sea, she pictured him lying on the deck of a sailboat that fitted him as loosely and smoothly as his dinner jacket. She could see him handling the tiller expertly with his toes; his exquisite plum sheen proclaiming an unshakable kinship to the sun, the sea and the isle.

That evening he put on the new jacket; and off they went, arm in arm, to the palm-roofed dining pavilion of her dream. It was dimly lit, a small hurricane lamp flickering on each table. The palms swayed to Calypso music. The scene was quietly festive, like a painting slowly coming to life. There were the newly arrived pale people from the States, anticipating tomorrow's sun and next week's tan. There, also, were those who had already spent many lazy days on the beaches; their watercolor tans were pastel patches against the oil-brown native waiters, who navigated skillfully among the white tablecloths. The stage was perfectly set for her beautifully jacketed husband to enter and take his place in her dream.

Several white couples converged behind them in the dining room entrance. Suddenly, a bill was pressed into her husband's hand. A man whispered confidentially, with the greatest of urgency, "A good table for my party, if you would."

Her husband, hand extended, stared at the bill. A second bill was placed on the first. The man leaned forward as insistently as before. "I know you can take care of it," he whispered. "Please."

She and her husband stood looking at each other, stunned momentarily and speechless. Later they would laugh about it, but at the moment of comprehension they could not.

The brown headwaiter glided toward them, beckoning. Her husband pressed the bills back into the insistent one's palm, saying evenly, "You've made a mistake."

As they turned to follow the headwaiter, only she noticed the crimson flush that swept the insistent one's face. Her husband undoubtedly was too occupied with his own complex emotions, which registered not at all through the coconut-shell brown of his features. She loved the way her husband looked.

Dear Son,

Among the hodgepodge of picket lines that militant blacks are marching on these days—protesting this and demanding that—there is one kind that the Tall Lady and I find hard to resist: Any picket line that calls attention to the fact that black men desperately need access to better-paying jobs. Which is my excuse and hers for having carried you in our arms on a protest march today.

It was a clear violation of a house rule: Our son will make his own decisions about such things as picket lines, politics, churches and military service. He is free to embrace any of those, some or none at all. We hope that we are wise enough to teach him to understand his choices.

As for today's violation of that rule—we felt that you were still too young to be affected one way or the other. And besides, this picket line sprang up out of the black, so to speak; we came upon it by chance, and joined it on an impulse. There was scarcely time to find a reliable baby-sitter.

The three of us were driving through Harlem, returning from a brief holiday at the summer house fifty-five miles out of town. There, in the middle of the ghetto, we saw a crowd of black men and women. Perhaps a thousand. Some were carrying banners and homemade picket signs. We stopped to look, wondering what it was about.

An angry middle-aged black man in shirt sleeves was addressing the crowd through a loudspeaker on the sidewalk. He satisfied our curiosity, and proved once again how contagious anger is.

The city of New York was building a new hospital in Harlem, he said. Millions of tax dollars involved. A payroll that added up to tens of thousands of dollars every week. And the guys who were getting the money, the skilled workmen on the project—electricians, steamfitters, sheet-metal workers, plumbers and crane operators—were all white. Only one or two black men were on the job, the speaker said. Pushing shovels and wheelbarrows.

He said the city blamed the private contractors hired to build the hospital, the contractors blamed the unions, and the unions blamed black men for not having union cards.

We could sense what was growing in the crowd, growing in ourselves, what could have turned this street-corner rally into something wild and ugly.

But the speaker had other things in mind. He led the crowd to the construction site, two or three blocks away. We got out of the car and tagged along. There seemed to be no choice. He had told it like it was and we had heard speeches exactly like his so many times that we had come to accept it in principle. We were not worried about this or that detail because Mister Charlie had long ago forced us to believe in the substance. Which meant that the charge had evolved into something of a protest ritual.

The naked steel girders at the hospital site, painted a garish orange, were deserted. A fellow picket told us that the city had halted work on the project to avoid violent demonstrations, and to investigate the charges and counter-charges.

So we walked. We chanted slogans about justice and equality. We sang the familiar freedom songs. Around and around and around the four sides of the block. When my arms became too tired, I handed you over to the Tall

37

Lady. A couple of round trips later, she passed you back to me. It went on like that for three hours.

You seemed frightened at first—apparently upset by the fierceness of the chanting and the singing. Gradually you settled into one of your typical moods—the one the Tall Lady describes as "a mixture of acceptance and disapproval."

By then our backs were aching. Our feet were lumps of pain. And our son seemed to have put on weight—at least a metric ton. I thought of all the other places I would rather be, of all the other things I would rather be doing right then.

We gave up, exhausted. The other marchers also seemed in pain; but most of them kept going. Theirs was not a part-time commitment.

Back in the car, as we sped down the East River Drive —lusting for a couple of dry martinis—the Tall Lady summed up our defection.

"I could have kept going," she said sadly, "even with the pain in my back, if I only knew how many times I'd have to walk around that block to get one black man one job. Two hundred times. Even four hundred times; I would do it. But the way it was . . . it was something like swimming out to sea. No end in sight. No signs to tell you how much farther you have to go. No way to be sure that you're really moving ahead, and not kidding yourself in the grip of some subtle undertow."

Dear Adam,

Last night, my son, after you curled up in sleep, the Tall Lady and I drank more champagne than any *four* people ever should. Getting up this morning was an agony no human being should have to bear.

The champagne was a necessary element in a ritual, however. We were celebrating my official release from the United States military reserves. They can't send your daddy back into the service anymore.

Does that sound unpatriotic?

Good.

Patriotism has little chance of infecting my brain. It has already been ravaged by another disease. The memory, for example, of the time I went to Louisville, Kentucky, on furlough, wearing the uniform of what they told me was my country. I was stopped by some of my countrymen at the doors of a restaurant, a bar and a movie theater. All in the same block. In a span of fifteen minutes.

I was nineteen years old then. The patriotism bug never had a chance to bite me. It was drowned in Louisville in my tears of helpless rage.

And frankly, my son, I think I would rather see this country overrun by its enemies than fight to protect those of my countrymen who are certain someday to give you such a sample of their democracy.

Ironically, however, I am glad I spent twenty-four months in uniform. As long as I stayed on military property, it wasn't too bad. The Korean War was going on; but I didn't have to shoot at anyone, and no one shot at me. The service proved the one corner of this society where the rules and frustrations affect blacks and whites equally. For the most part, a man is a man in the service. His job, his earnings, his living conditions and his opportunities—as well as what respect he gets—are directly related to his personal abilities. Nothing else.

That is why so many black men are making careers of military service these days. To escape.

Your daddy hasn't escaped, being a devout civilian; but I have managed a little to protect myself, the Tall Lady and you by building a barricade of money. That's the stuff Mister Charlie's god is made of.

The world hasn't changed since your daddy's service. There is another war going on now, also in Asia, in Vietnam. And the reports of it that I broadcast almost nightly add up to another special irony for black men. Since most of the soldiers assigned to combat are the uneducated, the disadvantaged and the poor—the ones this country can best afford to lose—an unfair percentage of the guys getting killed fighting for somebody else's freedom are black.

Now I am fearful that unless the world changes one helluva lot, and damned soon, there will come a day when Mister Charlie orders my son to risk his life to take the blessings of democracy to other faraway places.

I wish I could tell you, point-blank, not to go—not to accept such an ironic risk. But frankly, my son, I am not at all sure that to tell you that would be right.

Dear Adam,

Even without a war, Mister Charlie will someday demand that you serve your country. Well, it won't be your country—at least not yet. But that's not the question here. The question is, once they get you into military service, how do you survive?

It requires serious planning long in advance. The first thing to do is remain in college as close to four years as possible. You can hold your local draft board at bay by enrolling in a part-time military training program called R.O.T.C.—Reserve Officers Training Corps—that most universities have. There are branches for the Army, Navy and Air Force. (The Marine Corps depends on volunteers, but no son of mine would be that stupid.) Usually, the R.O.T.C. people don't spend all that government money training you to get killed.

Even if you don't elect R.O.T.C., your three or four years in college will make the military brass less prone to try turning you into a killer. Sad experience with the likes of your daddy has taught them that any young man who has learned a few things about the world he lives in, and how to think for himself, naturally resists the notion of killing people.

The Navy didn't get its hands on my brain until two years after my graduation from college. By then, I could never pretend to feel anything more ferocious than embarrassment when the chief petty officer would make a mob of us growl like animals and charge a platoon of strawmen with naked bayonets. They wound up assigning me to a desk job, where I had less chance of infecting others.

For me that meant I would survive Mister Charlie's undeclared wars to defend somebody else's freedom. But I still had to survive the Navy.

The danger in the Navy—or any other branch of the military—is that they try to turn your brain into mush. They do it by treating every individual as if he were a drooling idiot, and by crowding his brain with their own unreal picture of reality. To maintain your self-respect as a human being and a reasonably civilized man, you have to score small victories over the system from time to time. Nothing treasonous, you understand. Just enough to show that your mind is still your own, just enough to balance some of the many defeats the system is bound to deal to you.

One of the greatest of your daddy's small victories came in boot camp. My training unit was attending what the Navy calls an information lecture—meaning Navy propaganda. The chief petty officer in charge told us that his topic for the day was "The Evils of Communism." Then, lest we get a few ideas of our own about that, he listed the evils on the blackboard.

1. No right to choose your own leaders.
2. No right to choose your own job.
3. Low pay.
4. No right to go on strike.
5. No right to vote on major issues affecting your life.
6. No right to choose where you live.
7. Fear of arbitrary punishment by superiors.
8. No right to privacy.

When the chief finished writing the list, he turned to face us and asked if we had any questions or comments.

42

I held up my hand.

He nodded.

"Well, sir," I began, "I think you must have left something out of that list; because the way it reads now sounds just like the Navy to me."

Dear Adam,

Upon meeting a white toddler near your own age this afternoon—a boy who I'm sure will one day be your friend—you did two things that made your daddy proud. Let me set the scene:

While the boy's mother was in the kitchen helping the Tall Lady prepare lunch, his daddy and I were drinking martinis in the living room and exchanging what-a-genius-my-son-is stories. You and Eric Junior were scrambling about our feet banging objects with delight.

Eventually, young Eric decided that he should bang you on the head with one of your plastic milk bottles. I was pleased to see that after the first blow you merely pushed his arm away as you yelled. When he did it a second time, I was equally satisfied that you let him have a strong open-handed stiff-arm on the mouth that dumped him on the seat of his pants. He cried and so did you. But for the rest of the afternoon the two of you played together like the civilized roughnecks you are. Without declaring war.

Later, Eric Senior and I turned our discussion to your futures.

"I don't want to push him," the boy's father said proudly, "but the way he takes things apart—I mean, he's unusually clever at it—I think Eric is going to be some kind of engineer. Maybe a space scientist or an astronaut. Like I said, though, we don't want to push him. He can be anything he wants."

I countered with a list of household gadgets that you have not only taken apart but also put back together, one way or another. I was playing the Daddies' Game. But my mind was otherwise occupied for most of their visit.

Eric Junior can be anything he wants, his father had said. And it had hurt.

He had said it innocently, of course. No comparison intended. I know this man. He is one of the finest human beings I have met.

Still, it hurt.

Once again I was bitterly aware of the nonsense world outside as I watched our sons in a serious romp. For now, in the toddling stage, the two of you were exactly like all potential men—grimy hands, destructive curiosities and diapers that probably needed changing. But the balance would gradually disappear—as you both grew taller—in the eyes of the world outside.

I imagined you and Eric Junior as young men, polished and eager, best foot forward, trying to build a dream. And facing the Establishment: The power blocs who run this country; who enforce the laws; who control the industries, the unions, the jobs, the schools and the places to live— those who decide whether this man or that deserves to have his dream come true.

Again it hurt.

So, to ease the pain of my vision I made a wish for each of you: That Eric Junior may somehow inherit his father's allegiance to the common-sense principles of fair play. And that you, my son, may somehow inherit your daddy's will and strength to go over, around or through the barriers of ignorance that will be put in your way.

Dear Adam,

Another of your daddy's illusions has just been destroyed; this time by the Tall Lady. Of all people.

As I was boasting to my best friend—your self-appointed Uncle Julian—that you have learned to say *daddy*, the Tall Lady interrupted to tell it like it is.

"Of course, Adam hasn't the foggiest notion of what *daddy* means," she said with a laugh. "I was reading a book about babies just the other day. And this expert says that when a baby first learns to say *mommy* or *daddy*, he thinks he's saying a magic word—like abracadabra—to make something pleasant happen. Something pleasant does happen, in fact. He gets a lot of attention. Mommy or daddy pats him on the head and makes a big fuss over him. As if he has done something . . . supercalifragilistic-expialidocious."

I was not convinced until she produced the book. I read the passage and the expert's credentials on the jacket.

So much for a father's self-deception.

"Well, all right," I conceded. "But I still like to hear my son say *daddy*. Whatever he may mean by that."

At this stage of my life I can let go of illusions without going to pieces. Not only do I expect to lose them, but I am even glad to. It's part of the never-ending process of learning and growing up.

It was not always so for me. I can remember bursting into tears in the boys' room on my very first day at Public School 4 in Milwaukee. I was five years old, flanked by five or six older boys lined up at the urinals.

46

"Where did you come from, youngster?" one of them asked me.

"The angels brought me from heaven," I replied. My tone suggested that surely everybody knew that.

Some of them laughed so hard they cried. Then they told me. I hadn't been brought by the angels as I had been told at home. They explained, crudely, the mechanics of the sex act—what my daddy had done to my mother. Not *with* her. *To* her.

Eventually, I stopped bawling. I simply had no more tears. But I was totally crushed—heartbroken for days.

On the other hand, I would certainly dislike being still under the impression, as a grown man, that I had been delivered by angels. The shock of your arrival by more conventional means might have unnerved me completely.

By the time I reached college, I was more prepared for such ordeals. Indeed, I was suspicious of the whole world. It seemed to be cluttered with illusions. Even so, when the combined wisdom of my freshman courses in anthropology, philosophy, ancient history and psychology convinced me that angels, gods and devils were the earthly inventions of men, I was so undone I needed several months of psychiatric treatment to recover. When the shock wore off, I discovered that I felt much freer. The world began to make sense. I could then accept and live by Christian principles —such as the Ten Commandments—because they were reasonable. Not because I was frightened of the eternal flames of hell.

Up until then, it seemed, my illusions had little to do with the way I looked at myself. Then, in my junior year, I met a black freshman girl named Lorraine Hansberry. I am certain, my son, that you will have learned all about

Miss Hansberry by the time you read this letter. All about her success as a Broadway playwright before she died at the age of thirty-four. Even now, schools and civic organizations have begun to emphasize black contributions to this society. Lorraine's gifts will surely impress you just as they did the world.

But getting back to our days as a steady couple at the University of Wisconsin—Lorraine and I developed a crush on each other almost at the moment we met. It might have evolved into something more if she had not been much wiser than I.

Although younger by two years, Lorraine had learned to see the world more as it really was. She spent every spare moment away from the classrooms trying to change it, working with student action groups. She was the only girl I knew who could whip together a fresh picket sign with her own hands, at a moment's notice, for any cause or occasion. My concerns were more selfish. Like taking her sailboating in a rented snipe on Lake Mendota. Or just sitting under a tree holding hands and kissing. That was my idea of student action.

One day, under my favorite tree, she said for the umpteenth time, "Don't you ever think about what's going on around you?"

"I'd rather think about putting my arms around you," I replied wittily.

Then she told me. "Black people have too much to do to spend a lot of time on that. Don't you feel anything about all the discrimination that's going on?"

I explained that I knew all about it, but had found out that discrimination mainly was what happened to Negroes who couldn't compete with whites. "And I know damned well I can compete."

48

"What you're saying," Lorraine said patiently, "is that you think you're better than Negroes who haven't been to college. You haven't stopped to think about the reasons they haven't been—about the tremendous odds against them, and who sees to it that the odds don't change. The truth is you're not better than those Negroes.

"It's just that in the things that touch *their* lives, Mister Charlie has been so much worse."

Dear Adam,

That light-skinned black man who calls himself your Uncle Julian, your daddy's best friend, dropped in again this Saturday morning to tease us both. The Tall Lady was away taking a ballet class.

Your Uncle Julian playfully ridiculed my dream that you will one day be a triple-threat all-star quarterback.

"I know a thing or two about football myself," he said, stroking his chin. "From the way this boy is built, I'd say he was line material. A tackle maybe."

I think we won the day, however, when—on my signal —you picked up your undersized football with one hand and cocked your arm in the picture-book quarterback pose.

"Maybe that rascal *is* quarterback material," Julian conceded with unsuppressed admiration. "But if he is, he'll be the fattest quarterback they've ever seen in the Ivy League."

Later, when you dozed off for your pre-lunch siesta, Julian and I plunged into a bottle of Scotch and one of our favorite running debates. He tries to convince me that I should cure myself of the madness that stops me from voting in any election. On the other hand, I try to persuade him to give up that part of his madness that makes him bristle with indignation and spit insults at anyone who calls him a Negro.

"That's not only mad," I said, "it's ridiculous. There's nothing wrong with the word *Negro*. The thing that's wrong is the negative connotation Mister Charlie has in mind when he says it or thinks it. But Mister Charlie would have the same negative idea if he learned to call you by some other name. Afro-American, for example. You've heard that old joke about the black man who put a razor at a white man's throat and demanded that he be shown more respect; and the white man, badly frightened, showed more respect by calling him *Mister* Nigger."

Julian laughed, but he was still adamant. "I reject the term *Negro*," he explained, "because it is inaccurate. Something Mister Charlie made up. I want to be recognized as a person of some African ancestry and a few other strains of humankind as well."

"Very good," I said. "It sounds quite accurate. And scholarly. But how are you going to get all that into the little box marked 'Race' on your driver's license?"

We laughed at ourselves and filled the glasses again.

"The black man who can't laugh at himself is really in trouble," he said.

"I'll drink to that," I answered. And we did.

Between us, we recalled other laughable examples of the bizarre extremes blacks have been driven to by the climate in Mister Charlie's backyard.

Each of us knew two or three ex-playmates who had crossed over into "God's country"; that is, they were now passing for white. Some pretending to be bigots as well.

"Do you think that's good or bad?" Julian asked. "Passing, I mean."

I shrugged. "Who knows? Each black man has to work out his own arrangement with Mister Charlie. You survive as best you can, I suppose."

We also laughed about the Negro magazine *Ebony*, preaching "black pride" in its editorial pages while filling its pages with ads for products guaranteed to lighten dark skin and straighten kinky hair.

Julian told of a black man and wife, both schoolteachers,

who pretend they are French. Not in public; just in the microscopic world that is all their own, their apartment in the Harlem ghetto. Within those walls, they speak only French to each other. Almost perfect French after years of playing that game. All of their books are written in French. Their walls are decorated with reproductions of famous French paintings. And they spend their vacations in France.

"Well, don't keep me guessing," I said. "Do they play French games in the bedroom?"

We laughed and drank a toast "to the free French."

We also laughed about a black sorority, which, during our college days many years ago, would not accept girls with dark-brown skins.

"I understand, though," said Julian, "that since the Black Revolution began a few years ago that policy has changed. Now it's fashionable to be a black girl. And kinky African hair styles are becoming more popular every day."

He then told of a very dark-skinned woman who recently confessed to him that she had married her husband mainly because of his light skin, even though he was an obnoxious oaf. At the time, though, before the Black Revolution, she needed his light skin to make herself less black in her own eyes, a kind of proof that in spite of her dark skin she was not one of this society's untouchables. But now that the climate has changed in the black community—that is, Mister Charlie's evaluation is being accepted less and less—the lady wants out. She is reluctant to get a divorce because of the three children. But if anything should ever happen to her light-skinned oaf, "Hallelujah!" she'd say, and pick a second husband for what kind of man he is inside his skin. Where it counts.

I was reminded of an experience I had ten or twelve years ago with a black friend's six-year-old son in my hometown, Milwaukee. My friend Harry regarded me as something of an expert on psychology because I had spent four years at the state university in Madison.

"Boy, am I glad to see you," Harry said anxiously, pumping my hand at the door as I arrived at his house one evening. "I wish you would talk with Junior. That boy has got it into his head that he's white, and I can't convince him any different."

I laughed. It seemed to be a simple delusion, easily exposed. After all, Harry, his wife and Harry Junior were as dark as I am.

"Oh, I think we can straighten that out in a few minutes or so," I said.

Perhaps half an hour later, at what I thought the right moment, I began sneaking up on Junior. The trick was to catch him off guard. I began by asking him about school and how he liked it. Then I sprang my little trap.

"How many other Negroes are there in the class aside from you?" I asked.

"I'm not a Negro," he said evenly, but with a trace of hostility, I thought. "I'm white. But we do have three or four Negro kids in my class."

I suggested as casually as I could that he was mistaken, that he couldn't possibly be white, because his skin was just like his daddy's and mine; and we were certainly Negroes.

With a shy grin, Harry Junior said seriously, "Aw, you must be teasing me. My daddy is no Negro. And you neither."

I was ready to give up. "How on earth could you possibly think we're anything else but Negroes?" I asked.

"A Negro," he said, as if reciting, "is somebody who is black and dirty and ugly, and smells bad and talks bad, and has big feet and nobody likes him."

I really did give up then.

Harry Junior couldn't tell me where he had learned that definition. But he didn't have to. I knew it was in the air he breathed.

When I finished telling that story to your Uncle Julian, he laughed and wondered aloud, "What ever happened to Harry Junior? Did he ever learn?"

"Well, from what they tell me now," I said, "young Harry holds the rank of block captain in something called the Black Commandos. They're the ones you see so much of these days in the television newsreels. Leading marches into white neighborhoods night after night to demand open housing in Milwaukee."

Dear Adam,

Once again, my son, I have watched you approach a milestone. In a sense, the most significant of all the milestones that human beings reach.

We were lounging outdoors—the Tall Lady, you and I —among the whispering green trees and deep shadows that surround our summer house in the country. Gradually, moment by moment, as the three of us sat beside the swimming pool, some of the deeper shadows turned before our eyes to a silvery shade of pale. The sky hung low, crowded and alive with brilliant stars.

In the cradle of the Tall Lady's arms, you turned your eyes to the glowing wonders above. You sat very still for a very long time—not breathing at all, or so it seemed.

Observing your enchantment, we too sat still, remembering our own sense of awe.

Finally, you raised a chubby hand—reaching out to touch the nearest star. And then, though you have learned to say more definite words than any one-year-old should know, your questions in a small croaking voice were fragments of words not yet fully learned.

You were recognizing for the first time perhaps the deepest mystery of all. Neither the Tall Lady nor I could explain that mystery to you, my son. We can't even explain it to ourselves. This much I can tell you, however: That mystery, which is still in your mind as you read this twelve years later, is the basis of all things that men may call religion.

One of the wiser men of my time has defined religion as

the natural desire in the breast of every man to relate himself in a meaningful way to the universe.

That explains why, thousands of years ago, cavemen made gods of thunder and lightning. You see, my son, all religions basically represent the fumbling explanations of men through the ages who one day looked up at the stars. They could not help wondering, just as you wondered, "What has all that up there to do with me?"

Your daddy does not have the answer. But I feel deep in my bones that it is terribly important now and then to wonder.

Dear Adam-Smasher,

As you charged into your fifteenth month today—with your usual rough and tumble—you also advanced another notch on the human scale from savage toward civilized man.

The Tall Lady and I had taken you with us on a dinner visit to your Uncle Julian's and Aunt Mary's apartment. We had barely taken off our coats when you spotted three wall sockets in their living room. You toddled around the room, pointing to each socket—but not touching a single one—while trying to explain what you knew about them. Your vocabulary was still too meager for the subject. But your meaning was clear: You had learned from the recent experience of jamming a key into a wall socket in our apartment that wall sockets anywhere can make trouble.

"That boy," I crowed, "has a real sense of occasion. He's fourteen months old today, and he's proving it."

If you can learn to apply your reasoning, my son, you will be one up on Mister Charlie. I find again and again that he is largely incapable of looking at me on television and drawing the conclusion I have tried to lead him to for years: That since my black skin in no way lessens my ability to compete inside one of his jealously guarded sanctuaries, chances are that other black men could do the same.

This week, for instance, I received a long-distance phone call from a white acquaintance in New Orleans. Let's call him Larry Gump. He is a big wheel in the news dapartment of a television station there, in that part of the South my daddy used to call "the land behind the sun." We had met perhaps five months ago while working on the same special assignment in Chicago.

First, Larry wanted to know if I would consider leaving New York to broadcast news on his station in New Orleans. He could guarantee a substantial raise.

"Thanks for asking, Larry," I said. "But I don't think New Orleans is ready for me. I know I'm not ready for New Orleans."

He laughed. "I know what you mean. I just thought I'd ask on the off chance that you might agree with us down here that it's time this station put a Negro on the air. I couldn't think of anybody but you. We think it would help improve race relations."

I was slightly annoyed. It seemed that every white liberal in the country wanted to integrate the same small handful of black men over and over again. What about the other 21,999,900? In recent weeks, before Larry's call, I had been offered jobs as a baseball broadcaster in Cleveland, as an assistant press secretary for the Mayor of New York City, John V. Lindsay, and as an assistant press secretary for Senator Robert F. Kennedy.

"Larry," I said as patiently as possible for me, "if your station really wants to do something about race relations, why don't you hire a black man who is not already established in New York? Why not think in terms of increasing black participation? Why don't you hire a black man right there in New Orleans?"

There was a long pause while Larry digested those heresies.

58

"Well," he said uncertainly, "we want somebody who's terrific on the air—a finished newsman like you."

My patience was beginning to crumble. But here was a white man, I thought, who just might be able to understand something simple and obvious.

"Larry," I began, "there are two points I want you to think about carefully. First, I wasn't terrific, as you say, when I was hired by this station. And neither were you probably when you were first hired for television. Both of us had to be trained, the same as everybody else. In the second place, there are white broadcasters on the air in New York City and New Orleans who are not as good as either you or I. But they are on the air, even though they're mediocre. I don't know how to make this any plainer, Larry, except to say that what this whole racial thing is about is that black men should also have the right to be mediocre."

Another long pause in New Orleans. Larry Gump might be thinking, I guessed. Maybe I should give him the clincher.

I mentioned the name of a well-known broadcaster in the Midwest who was a black man. "Did you know," I asked, "that he was trained right here at my station in New York? Without even having a college degree?"

"You're kidding me," Larry said. "That guy's damned good."

"Then it stands to reason," I said, "that television broadcasting is not so tough to learn that everybody in it has to be born knowing how to look into a camera lens. A lot of people can do it. And some of those people—if given a chance—are black."

"Well, I'll be damned," Larry said. He was clearly surprised, but not the least bit angry. "I really never thought of it quite like that before."

We wished each other the best of everything, then said good-by.

Dear Adam,

Some letters ago, my subject was the wonders of creation, and the birth of gods in the minds of men. It occurs to me tonight that a postscript is in order about the popular but rarely stated concept of God in this society: A senile old white man with a long gray beard, full of pranks and caprices, busy around the clock pushing buttons and pulling levers to make the rain fall and protect the working girl, while answering an invisible telephone, and watching all men and all sparrows without the aid of television monitors.

Well, if that god exists, I can tell you, as one of his ex-disciples, that he does absolutely nothing for believers who happen to be black.

Dear Son,

In the middle of my newscast this evening, a copy boy rushed into the studio with a bulletin. The dateline was New Orleans, "that land behind the sun."

A few moments later, as I raised my gaze to the camera lens and informed my corner of the world all about it—perhaps four million people, I am told—I wished that there really was a Devil in hell to make a bargain with. I would sell my soul for a guarantee that you, my son, would never have to face this horror—unstated but real:

"This bulletin just in. A Federal Court in New Orleans has just reached an important verdict. It ruled that an amusement park in Baton Rouge, Louisiana, had a legal right to stop two Negro children and their mother at the gate, and refuse to let them in. The three judges on the panel said amusement parks like this one are not covered by the Federal Civil Rights Act, which forbids racial discrimination in places open to the general public. This particular park, they said, does not offer any public exhibitions or spectacles."

Dear Adam,

There are moments of fantasy in my life when there really is a Devil. He sometimes appears in my den late in the evening, complete with tail and pitchfork, lusting for my soul. He wears a bright red skintight suit, a red cloak and a stubby set of horns above his brow. His angular ruddy features seem permanently creased with a smirk. His voice is oily, confident, slightly effeminate. And he knows an easy mark when he sees one.

"I daresay," he begins coolly, "that you and I, sir, can do a deal."

I settle back in my leather chair and light my pipe. The Devil's dark eyes, drawn to the flame, suddenly glaze. For a long moment the angles in his face are diffused in a flush of ecstasy. Seeing that, I snuff out the match with as much defiance as I can muster.

"Feel free to strike another at any time, old chap," he says lightly, resuming his devilish smirk. "You know I'm hooked on the stuff."

I figure he's trying to put me off guard by pointing up a weakness. To hell with it, I tell myself. I'll ignore it.

"What kind of deal you got in mind?" I ask between deep pulls on my pipe.

"Oh, come come," he says with mock impatience. "You know perfectly well I wouldn't even be here if you hadn't been wishing for something quite specific with all your—ah—soul."

My skin is too dark to blush. But the Devil can see what is in my eyes. He knows he's got his man. He chuckles briefly.

"I suggest," he resumes smoothly, "that we get on with it without delay—to our mutual advantage, I might add. After all, I do have other appointments, you know."

I exhale a cloud of smoke very slowly, resigning myself to what I know has to be. However, I haven't lost my wits altogether. "All right," I say warily. "I know what you want from me. But what are your terms?"

Gently, the Devil props his pitchfork against the wall. Then, facing me directly, he brings the tips of his ruddy fingers together, forming a tent in front of his lips—a burlesque of piety.

"My dear fellow," he purrs, "the terms are exactly as you dictated in your wish." Here, he produces two scrolls —an original and a carbon copy—as if by magic from the inner folds of his cloak. "We needn't bother with the preamble," he mumbles as he scans the document from the top. "All it covers is the standard whereas and wherefors. . . . Ah, here we are. 'Granted that your son Adam Fitz-James shall live out his days as free in his mind as any man ever born. That he shall never feel even the slightest pain from any injustice or any indignity because of the color of his skin. That neither shall he feel denied of a single opportunity, punishment or reward because of said color. That he shall always feel confident that his triumphs and defeats are directly related to his merits. Guaranteed without reservation by His Satanic Majesty, et cetera, et cetera.' "

The Devil passes both copies of the contract to me, along with a ballpoint pen that seems to materialize in his fingers. "There. I believe that covers everything," he says graciously. "Now if you would just be good enough to sign both scrolls on the dotted line at the bottom."

"Not just yet," I tell him, scanning the document myself. "What about the escape clause? Aren't you supposed to give me at least a chance for a way out—to save my soul from hell?"

His chuckle is genuine amusement. Or so it seems. Absently, he retrieves his pitchfork and rests his chin on the center prong.

"Oh my," he says in a bored tone of voice, "you're all alike . . ."

Here, the Devil stops abruptly as he sees my hostile gaze. His manner becomes sober, apologetic. He realizes he has offended me.

"A thousand pardons, old chap," he says meekly, bowing deeply in my direction. "I didn't mean what you think— not that all *black* men are alike. I mean all *men* I meet who want to do a deal. A thousand, thousand pardons."

I am only partly mollified, however. "I also want it written into the contract," I demand, "that no person who meets my son shall ever commit a careless blunder like that to raise anxieties in his mind."

He nods his chin vigorously above the point of his pitchfork. "Done, done," he agrees. He gestures casually with one hand in my direction. I can feel the scrolls growing inches longer in my hands. "Now, if you'll take a look at the new paragraph just above the line where you sign," he says, "you'll find your last request covered exactly as you dictated."

I skip down to that paragraph and read it carefully. On both copies. I know this guy is full of tricks. But I find that it's all spelled out in the last paragraph just the way I demanded it. Okay.

"Now, about that escape clause you mentioned," the Devil says. "I'm afraid you've been reading the kind of stories that always place me in the worst possible light. You don't seem to understand that I am rendering a valuable public service on a *quid pro quo* basis. In point of fact, sir, I have offered only one escape clause in my entire career—in the very first contract I handled. I'm sure you can appreciate that my board of directors ordered a change of policy after that sad experience. Now, why don't you just sign and let me get on to other poor souls in need."

I check the last paragraph again and sign both copies with his pen.

"Under the terms of this policy then," I say, "I take it that I cannot hope to escape the fires of hell?"

His nod is diplomatic, barely perceptible. And, somewhat self-consciously, he conceals his pitchfork under his cloak. But I can see his long fingers twitching to get a grip on the scrolls I am still holding. This makes me a bit suspicious.

"There is no need for you to dwell on the—ah—payment," he says soothingly. "Not at all. You can think instead about how your son will be enjoying life—feeling free and untroubled—as few black men in your society dare dream of."

That settles it. But wait—I pull back the scrolls just before they reach his grasping fingers.

"Just a cotton-picking minute," I say. "I just realized you keep talking about how my son will *feel* about his life. Not about how his life will *be*. Unless you guarantee that his life will *be* all the things I wished, this deal is off."

The Devil sighs.

"My dear fellow," he begins, his voice dripping remorse and conciliation. "Now you are asking me to change the world. That was not in your original wish, nor," he con-

66

tinues, rushing past the objection I want to make, "is it entirely within my, ah, realm.

"Although I cannot guarantee that he will never meet one of those chaps you are fond of calling Mister Charlie, cannot guide him between the raindrops, so to speak, I *can* guarantee that he will not feel wet. The details are *my* job as the wishing is yours. And in doing my job, I have taken full account of the fact that he will be living among thousands of those chaps. After all, an intelligent man like you knows as well as I that they are almost everywhere."

"Okay, okay. I know the problem," I say impatiently. "The question is what kind of a double-crossing deal did you have in mind?"

"I do wish you wouldn't put it quite that way," he says, looking pained. "This is just a matter of tedious operative details. Nothing you need concern yourself about. Now, if you will just give me my copy—"

"Where's the fire?" I interrupt without listening to my own words, for I have now begun to unroll the scroll again to look for those tedious operative details. I find them buried in a paragraph of fine print. Slowly I read them.

And then I tear up the contract, both copies.

The Devil shrugs, smiles and bows deeply. A second later he vanishes in a cloud of acrid smoke.

I can still see that fine print before my eyes:

Whereas said son shall be living in a society rampant with a relentless racism that cannot help responding to his black skin, and whereas no black man in that society has ever escaped from the aforesaid racism, he shall be protected from mental anguish by the best available means; to wit, he shall be persuaded at an early age to accept painless unawareness through the generous use of marijuana, peyote, LSD, heroin and other drugs.

Dear Adam-Smasher,

From the way you cling to your stuffed blue dog with the black floppy ears—even when fast asleep—I suppose you will still remember "Puppy" at thirteen. But you probably will have forgotten the white man who gave it. He calls himself your Uncle Bruce.

Bruce is a handsome bachelor type, about the same age as your daddy. He works for an advertising agency on Madison Avenue; and we've been good friends for years.

Well, the day your Uncle Bruce came to see you a couple of weeks ago and brought Puppy, he asked me an unexpected question.

"I've been dating a terrific Negro girl," he said. "We're thinking about getting married. Do you think it's a good idea?"

I didn't blink an eye. But I didn't answer his question, either. Instead, since I loved him, I told him how to find his own answer.

"All I can say, Bruce, is that marriage can be a trying business even when man and wife are the same color. The thing the two of you have to decide between yourselves is whether what you feel for each other is strong enough to stand the extra problems. I mean the stares, the insults and fist fights, coming at you from both sides—black and white.

"Now you might get a clue," I told him, "if you begin taking your black girl friend to all the places you normally like to go."

I had assumed, quite correctly, that their dating so far

had been extremely careful—limited to certain people and places that they felt they could possibly trust. That meant they spent most of their time in bed. Your daddy went down that road many years ago.

Well, your Uncle Bruce dropped in again this evening, two weeks later, and told me how the experiment worked out.

Luckily, he had been able to avoid the fist fights, he said, having the courage to walk away from challenges. But he and the girl had changed their minds, and parted as friends. Even without fist fights, he said, the pressure from both sides was unbearable.

Dear Son,

As you may have gathered from some of the things I've said, sex is a tricky preoccupation that can lead to all sorts of monkey business. Which a gentleman later regrets.

Until now I have held back on telling about the particular sex charade—enacted several times, I'm afraid—that your daddy regrets most of all.

It happened when your daddy was a sophomore in college—eighteen years old—still burning in the hell of puberty. Well, there was an organization on campus, sort of a bush-league Communist front, that gave house parties on the weekends. They were known as "racial mixers." Actually, they were heavy-handed Communist recruiting campaigns.

By mixing socially, dancing and drinking hard booze with blacks, Puerto Ricans, assorted orientals and Jews, these campus crusaders tried to prove whose side they were on.

If you were especially hard to convince, they would send in what I called their shock troops: pretty girls who would pretend to have a crush on you. Lovely creatures of the cause. They were sleek and sultry in a put-on sort of way. Limpid eyes in pale soulful faces. Wearing extra-tight bras that overemphasized the soft round promises in their sweaters.

Well, that was the kind of recruiting sergeants they often assigned to your daddy. It was a contest of wills and strategies. Which I nearly always won. At the proper moment I would suggest in one arch phrase or another that we

70

continue our discussion about the glories of the cause in bed.

To those who balked or tried to change the subject, I then asked my favorite question, with just the right boyish wistfulness:

"Is there any real difference between Communists and the rest of white society—I mean different from capitalist girls?"

It was like shooting fish in a barrel.

Unfortunately, many years went by before I grew wise enough to realize that I had been wrong. True, they had been trying to take advantage of my special problem while I succeeded in taking advantage of theirs.

But that is a justification that should not appeal to even a sophomore.

I am convinced now that deceit, in its various forms, is a root cause of the pervasive sickness of this society. Therefore, no civilized man can afford to condone it. For when men feel free to deceive one another, on any grounds, they do it. They lie, misrepresent, distort and otherwise cheat their own kind. And from such deceits and betrayals springs a terrifying array of other evils, as the deceived concentrate their energies on getting even, or simply joining in the fun.

Again, I am convinced now that what this society needs more than anything else is a crusade by individual men— each in his own dealings—against lies, deceits and misrepresentations.

There is no telling how tall a man might grow living in a climate of candor.

Dear Adam,

It is the conviction of every man I have met that he is beset by well-intentioned advisers who think they know what is best for him better than he knows himself. Your daddy is no exception.

Today I was beset by two dear friends, one black and one white.

First, I received a long-distance call from Milwaukee. One of my college roommates of twenty years ago offered to pay my plane fare and expenses if I would fly to Wisconsin the following week to lead a black protest march on the state capitol in Madison. He believed I was ideal for the role as a well-known black man; my presence would attract more public attention to the demonstration, and perhaps impress the power structure.

"Ike," I said, "I hate to disappoint you. I think a march on the state capitol is a fine idea. But to put it as plainly as I can, that simply is not my way. In my own way, I'm trying to do what little I can to help right here where I am. But it has to be my way. I'm sorry, but that's my rule."

I don't know if Ike is still my friend.

Later today, a white friend from my college days telephoned from New Jersey, Mrs. Meyers.

Would I serve as master of ceremonies at a parade in celebration of a worthy cause? She went on to say that her committee had decided that I was ideal for the job, and they were so sure I would accept—for the worthy cause—that they had gone ahead with publicity releases saying I would be there.

"I apologize for that," Mrs. Meyers said sincerely. "But I'm afraid now that unless you do accept, a lot of people may hold it against you. Oh, you know how some people are. They'll be saying you don't care, or something."

As gently as possible for me, I told Mrs. Meyers that although I talk a lot on television, I am not an emcee for parades; that I have no desire to become one; that my way of helping what I regard as worthy causes is to walk on an occasional picket line; to contribute a few dollars; and to speak informally with youngsters—black, white or in-between—on what I think is a reasonable approach to becoming sensible human beings. And, finally, that I have learned to set my own standards and follow my own judgment without worrying what others may think, so long as I know that I have not tried to offend them.

I don't know if Mrs. Meyers is still my friend either.

Dear Adam,

Having explained that your daddy is not in the front lines of the Black Revolution, I think a word may be in order about the private little wars I fight with Mister Charlie every day. Today I fought a major battle. The weapon of the enemies was familiar, but extremely powerful in this terrain—the office where I work. Ah, but they reckoned without your daddy's derring-do.

Without explanation I was summoned to the fifty-second floor. That's where the power structure of my company holds its councils of war. Never before had I reconnoitered that sanctified stronghold.

When I arrived, still wondering what kind of operation this might be, I found a dozen Mister Charlies waiting in ambush. More than that, they were clearly ready to annihilate the self I think I am; they were smiling.

The battle was joined with handshakes all around. There wasn't a man in the trenches, including your daddy, earning less than forty thousand dollars a year. We were not quite equals, however.

Then they told me. I had been chosen—I supposed by a vote—to represent our company at a job-opportunity conference in Jersey City. There was a lot of unrest over there, they said in a stuttering, roundabout way.

As a matter of fact, there is a lot of unrest everywhere. Only three days ago, I ignored an invitation to attend a job-opportunity conference at the White House. The telegram was signed "Hubert H. Humphrey, Vice President."

"Our company is very pleased to be participating in a conference like this," one of my adversaries said. "We think there should be more conferences like this in a lot of places where they are needed. Now. Where do you fit in? Well, you'll be stationed at a booth with visual exhibits and equipment that show what our company is all about. There'll be a lot of young fellows circulating among the various booths set up by a dozen corporations. A lot of young fellows from the minority groups, I might add. They'll be coming around to ask questions that you should have no trouble answering."

There was a long, embarrassing cease-fire. One dozen Charlies were waiting for my response. I couldn't help the silence; I was too choked with rage to talk.

Finally, I felt controlled enough to try a probing counterattack. Without four-letter words.

"Well, gentlemen," I said slowly, carefully, but a bit too fiercely. "If you're *telling* me I have to go to this job-opportunity conference, I'll go. Frankly, I need this job I've got. But if you're *asking* me about going, then I say I want nothing to do with it."

There was another ominous silence over the foxholes. I looked at my bosses around the perimeter. Twelve good men and true. Their smiles had been replaced by reddening masks of astonishment. There was nothing about this situation in the field manual.

As for me—I was just plain angry and scared. They could wipe me out right there.

Dimly, in some barely accessible region of my mind, I realized that I should have softened my answer. Not my position, but my answer. I should have given them some indication of my deep involvement with my job in their company, my sense of allegiance and belonging, my appreciation for their giving me a rare opportunity for self-expression and self-fulfillment. It was also true that since joining the company, I had never had a feeling—until that job-conference summons—that I was being misused or exploited in any way. Not for a moment.

These men had met me on my own terms. I had not been hired to be a Negro reporter. As a matter of fact, I had been hired before they knew the color of my skin. One of them had admired some of my by-line writing in *The New York Times*, and called to offer me a job as a radio news writer. Furthermore, once I accepted the job, they treated me no differently from white writers hired about the same time.

All of us fledglings had been dumped into "the pool." Which meant writing half a dozen news scripts a day, or night, for other people to read on the air. It was the lowest rung in the business. We were told, in effect, that with luck, hard work, devotion to duty and to deadlines, we could work our way up to writing for television. After that, they said, with more luck, et cetera, we might work our way up to street reporter for radio or TV. And after that, with more et cetera, we might wind up as broadcasters! Hallelujah! With maybe a five-minute news show of our own.

They had seemed to be in no hurry at all to advance me or anyone else in the pool. Which was frustrating at times. But I did have the feeling that my black skin, a handicap most of my life, might now work to my advantage. It would be poetic justice.

That is not how it worked out.

It took me the better part of a year to make the grade

in radio writing, and advance to writing for television. There was a great deal I had to learn about editing film and video tape, mixing sound, mixing film and tape, interlocking film with separate sound tracks, projecting two reels of films at the same time, and much more. I learned by asking questions about the things I didn't understand. And by reading books about film and video tape and what makes television work.

Even with concentrated effort, however, it took about a year and a half to qualify as a full-time street reporter. Now I had to learn how to direct the shooting of film at the scene of news events, how to compete with other bird dogs in the street in mass interviews, and much more.

After two years and nine months, I got a nightly fifteen-minute newscast, having filled in occasionally on five-minute TV news shows beforehand. Now I had to learn how to speak all over again. That meant elocution lessons, breathing exercises, memory exercises and, again, much more. It was hard work. The hardest phase perhaps was learning to put together a compact yet comprehensive, understandable and entertaining news package. And supervising writers, production assistants, film editors and videotape editors working with me.

Then, after four and a half years with the company, I was promoted to half-hour newscasts. The hard work continued, and I found still more to learn.

In all that climb, I was never anything less than a general-assignment working stiff, never anything less than my colleagues. I was not fenced in or fenced out of news assignments, whether the subject was politics, murder, civil rights, disaster or beauty queens. When any assignment came up, if I was the man on deck, I covered it.

And there were times when I had reason to bitch and swear like everyone else about our common grievances— long periods of ridiculous nighttime hours, extra shifts on what was supposed to be a day off, and working with borrowed equipment in the office. It took me four and a half years to get a desk and a typewriter of my own.

All of this, disappointments as well as triumphs, had given me a sense of belonging. Also, a sense of having achieved a measure of fame and fortune on merit, not through somebody's charity. The money was damned good, too. And I was proud in the knowledge that my regular nightly appearances on the screen—talking about anything and everything—served to reinforce in literally millions of black people a belief that all black people harbor deep down: Anything they can do, we can do as well—if only they'll give us the same chance.

But all that is what I *should* have told that formidable array of company executives in refusing to go to Jersey City. During our tense confrontation, I suppose, none of those sentiments could break through my wall of resentment.

As the silence deepened in the room, I realized that it was too late now to retreat. I had told them flatly that I wanted no part of their so-called job-opportunity conference. And since retreat was out of the question, your daddy charged again.

"Furthermore," I said quietly, resigned to the worst, "I resent the whole idea right down to my toes. In the first place, I don't have any jobs to give. It seems to me that the people who do the hiring for this company are the ones to go. That's the only way to convince minorities that you mean business. Not just playing another game. It doesn't mean a thing to send a black example.

"And I resent being regarded as some kind of freak all of a sudden. To be trotted out on exhibit when it suits somebody else's purposes. I am not a freak. I am a man. I am a full-time employee of this company, and I'm doing a competent job. If I'm not, I should be fired."

Well, they didn't fire your daddy; and I have the feeling that nothing further will be said about my going to Jersey City or anywhere else. Except on regular news assignments.

As it always happens in your daddy's little combats, the world hasn't been changed. But I like to think that there are twelve more Charlies in the world who are beginning to understand this: Equal opportunity has nothing to do with conferences. What it's about is simply filling a job with the first capable man who comes along.

Dear Son,

As a rule, Adam-Smasher, I try to discourage you from answering the telephone. You seem to regard it as a fascinating toy for grownups. When I pry it from your chubby, determined grip, rejecting your angry but nonviolent protests, I remind myself that nothing annoys me more than phoning another grownup and having his infant menace answer with what strikes my ears as gibberish.

But early this evening when it rang, I was in the bathroom; and you, my son, won the race. Though not for long.

It turned out to be an important call. Aunt Letty was calling from Detroit. I don't remember her exact words; I was too traumatized. I do remember that for perhaps the first time since I have known the old girl she did not once blame anything on Confucius.

As Aunt Letty was talking with me, she was lying on the floor of her ghetto apartment in the darkness—pinned down by gunfire from a riot raging in the streets. I could hear the whine of bullets and their screeching ricochets. The bark of distant guns and the crash of broken windows also punctuated her conversation. A helluva time to be phoning. But Aunt Letty's voice was calm and deliberate. She told me how much she loved me, that she was counting on me to keep the *hui* going no matter what, and that she planned to leave a little something for you, my son, in her will.

Then suddenly, in the middle of a sentence, the line went dead. It was then that I realized exactly what was on Aunt Letty's mind. I did not try to stop my tears.

She was calling to say goodbye just in case.

Dear Adam,

Nearly all of my television newscast tonight was about black violence and destruction. The sporadic Black Revolution is erupting this week in Brooklyn, Jersey City, Newark, Philadelphia, Detroit, Milwaukee—that's where your daddy grew up—and Cincinnati.

Right now, my son, you are much too young to understand it. But someday, I imagine, you might want to ask: "What did you do in the Black Revolution, daddy?"

Well, up to now your daddy has done next to nothing. And I feel some guilt about it. The Black Revolution is being fought by other men, aroused to risking their lives by the same black agony that has driven me.

My daddy never really lived
before he died
He could never count on justice
or know a free man's pride
And now it's almost certain
that I, too, will be denied
I've got to make things better
for my son and for my tribe

Dear Son,

Ordinarily, nothing stirs more anxiety in your daddy's heart than the sound of my Adam-Smasher crying. Tonight, however, there was an exception. I was grateful for your tears.

You cried out in the darkness—not because of anything serious, I am glad—but because you were apparently having a nightmare. That's my guess because, happily, you woke me from a nightmare of my own. You accepted the reassurances of my shoulder and soon went back to sleep. But I was still too shaken by my dream. I needed a drink. And time to reassure myself.

The events of my nightmare were almost completely familiar—things I often dream of wide awake. I daydream of being the Black Commando. A one-man riot at large. I imagine myself setting off miniature nuclear explosions to cripple the white power structure. I blow up the things that hit Mister Charlie where he lives—in the money belt. U.S. Steel, General Motors, A. T. & T.—all of the corporate giants of Christendom. Boom! Boom! Boom! And the whole state of Mississippi. Pow!

From my supersonic jet fighter, I drop leaflets that warn Mister Charlie of further destruction unless he meets this simple demand: Behave yourself.

In my daydream, Mister Charlie wants to go slowly, gradually. He begs me to be patient. But finally, when my bombs have almost wrecked the entire economy and Wall Street itself has been blasted to rubble, he comes around. At first he plays fair and behaves himself only out of fear.

Then because he knows it is the law. And finally because he knows it is right.

That's how it works in my daydream—perfectly. No bloodshed at all. Not even when I blow up the state of Mississippi. But in the nightmare, something went terribly wrong. My bombs brought massive slaughter in the night. To the just and the unjust. To blacks and whites. It was ghastly. It was real. There was even a smear of blood on the moon.

When you roused me from that nightmare, my relief that I hadn't really done those things was boundless. Does that mean I wish someone else would play the Black Commando and take responsibility for the bloodshed?

Your daddy is not as crazy as all that.

Dear Adam,

The Tall Lady and your daddy are quite merry and mellow tonight—the effects of two bottles of champagne during a private celebration at home. We received another phone call from Detroit. Aunt Letty lives!

Despite the riot and the shooting, that grand old girl has survived.

Today, she said, things are getting back to normal. In the course of our conversation, she told me what *normal* often means.

Early this morning, she said, she found a white delicatessen just a few blocks from her apartment in the ghetto. It had somehow been spared during the four days and four nights of violence. The Come-and-Get-It Delicatessen. It had not received any deliveries for four days, however, and much of the unpackaged food had spoiled. Even so, there were customers in the store, mostly black.

While Aunt Letty was carefully examining a bin of soggy tomatoes, she overheard a white woman in the next aisle complain to the butcher behind the counter. "What on earth do you mean putting meat as bad as this on display? Can't you see it's completely ruined? Not fit to eat?"

She was indignant, Aunt Letty said. But the white butcher was not upset. "Look, lady," he said quietly, "this meat is not for you. It's for the others. And let's face it, I've got to make a living and they don't know any better. Believe me, those people are just like pigs." He laughed out loud, Aunt Letty said.

Upon hearing that laugh—she described it as the mating call of vultures—Aunt Letty stepped around the corner

84

and into the aisle that ran past the butcher's counter. She picked up a jar of pickles from the nearest shelf and deliberately smashed it to the floor before his eyes. Without a word she marched out, and kept on marching—nearly thirteen blocks, she said, in the rain—until she found another store.

Later in the day, she told me, there had been a faculty meeting at the small college where she teaches, well beyond the ghetto. They had to decide, among other things, which students had done well enough in the summer term to be graduated.

When the name of one of the Negro girls in the class came up, Aunt Letty recalled that the girl's grades were terrible. She was an eager child, but she just didn't have what it takes to be a teacher. Aunt Letty said so when her turn came to give an appraisal of Betty Lou. "In my opinion," she said, "Betty Lou is simply not qualified for the responsibility of teaching."

But there was unexpected, well-intentioned dissent from four of her colleagues, Aunt Letty said. For the wrong reasons. Finally, the faculty chairman—described by Aunt Letty as a sweet old ninny—made the decision: "I feel that although Betty Lou's grades are not too good," the sweet old ninny said sweetly, "she's a very serious and dedicated person. I think that we can safely make an exception in her case. Besides, she once told me that she plans to teach at that nice colored college they have down South—the one in Tuskegee. I think that under the circumstances, we should give this dear child a helping hand."

A helping hand? Don't they know any better than that?

Aunt Letty was almost undone, she said. "Confucius say if these be friends, may my enemies live to be a hundred."

It was much later in the day, she said, after her eyes had

cried themselves dry, that she recovered from that faculty meeting. Besides the suffocating rage she had felt over what they were about to send to Tuskegee—and why—there was also the awful feeling, she said, that the bottom had dropped out of her world. If they could lower their standards of competence for a girl like Betty Lou, did that also mean that they had made allowances to give her a job on the faculty? Was she incompetent? A showcase black to prove that the staff was integrated?

"It finally came to me just before I called you," Aunt Letty said, "that I would never know the answer to those questions. No black person in this country can ever know. One way or another, they raise the same question in every black mind, sooner or later. So I made up my mind that being black I can't afford to depend on their picture of me for my sense of worth and integrity. I'll have to supply that myself. All by myself. As for those questions about whether I am qualified or simply being tolerated or shown off—well, all I can do, in whatever black-white situation I am in, is to bring as much personal integrity as I can to it as it comes. And never demand anything on the basis of my black skin alone. Confucius say he who see himself with honest eye give no weight to foolish guess by stupid enemy."

Dear Aunt Letty had survived it all once more.

Dear Adam,

Aunt Letty called again from Detroit this morning—
cackling and giggling hysterically—happier than I have
ever known the old girl to be. There was a brief flare-up
of violence in the ghetto last night, she said. Nothing
serious. Just one store attacked by vandals and burned to
the ground: the Come-and-Get-It Delicatessen.

And she added, inevitably, "Confucius say man who
laugh loud also cry very hard."

Dear Adam,

Even if black men burn down every building in the fifty states, Mister Charlie will still make changes in this society with grudging gradualism. It's the best he can do. And his changes will not be enough to promise a single day of complete equality in my lifetime or yours.

But change there is, and compared with, say, the last hundred years, the pace is quickening. Partly out of enlightenment, mainly out of guilt and fear. By the time you are seventeen years old, in 1983, you will find an America slightly improved over the one I've grappled with all my life.

From the start, my son, you will have had advantages that your daddy did not begin to enjoy until halfway between the womb and the grave. Judging from what the Tall Lady and I have now and our prospects, you are not likely to face a single day of poverty. We have several thousand dollars in the bank, we own valuable property in three cities and in one foreign country, we have long-term investments in your name, and we are members of a family *hui* with growing assets.

These guarantee that you will not have to start where most black boys start, in the ghetto. Frankly, the Milwaukee ghetto your daddy grew up in was not as bad as most. It's true that we—my daddy, Aunt Letty and I— had to wage constant war against rats and roaches, the plumbing was less than reliable, garbage pickups in our neighborhood were unreasonably slow, and our white slumlord didn't believe in dipping into profits for repairs. Even so, where we lived on Veliet Street was the nicest part of the ghetto. I've seen much worse this year in Harlem and the Bedford-Stuyvesant section of Brooklyn.

Also, we never went hungry, even if a dietician would have been appalled. Aunt Letty was going to night school and working as a cleaning woman by day at white homes in the suburbs. Most of my clothes were hand-me-downs from the families she worked for. My daddy had a series of menial jobs—working with picks and shovels and brooms and automobile tools. Their combined weekly income never exceeded seventeen dollars until Aunt Letty began teaching, in 1939, and my daddy went to work in a defense plant at the beginning of World War II.

I was relatively fortunate in one other way. Our family was a rarity, with only one child. Many families had five or six children. That meant not enough shoes to cover so many young feet and not enough food to fill so many young bellies.

I can remember many afternoons of walking with my barefoot playmates to the edge of the ghetto and watching white youngsters, from a distance, in the beautiful residential neighborhood that hemmed us in. Those kids had shoes. And more important, they had roller skates, bicycles, wagons, cowboy suits and a whole world of things that we could only simulate with odd pieces of junk, old broom handles and active imaginations. One of our favorite games was to pick a particular white youngster that we could pretend to be, sharing from a distance his triumphs in the skating races, the wagon races or the chase in Cowboys and Indians. Theirs was the real world, we felt. Ours was only a shadow. And we knew it would never change.

That was the worst of the ghetto experience. And still is. It does something to a black boy's mind akin to shrinking it. I think I would rather die right now than continue living if I thought your life, my son, would also be like that.

But like I said, things are slowly changing. As black violence increases across this nation, so—ironic, perhaps, but true—will your freedom. That means, first of all, more and better jobs for black men. Mister Charlie is stepping up his search for clean-cut, safely married super black men to integrate—the blacker the better. Partly because he wants to advertise himself as a reformed sinner. Partly because he is learning to regard black skin as anti-riot insurance.

I am slightly envious of you and your generation, my son, when I recall that black skin had no value in Mister Charlie's world when I was growing up. I can remember that the few Negroes culled from the herd for token integration in those days had extremely fair skins. This created a light-skinned black elite. Which in turn created frictions and prejudices in the ghetto, a continuous pecking order with Mister Charlie at the top—unreachable and supreme. Divided as we were and crippled in spirit as he made us, we could not climb up in sufficient numbers to challenge him.

It was only a part of the "natural order" then that more than a few grown black men I knew tried to support their wives and children by shining shoes. It was also natural that I began my working career by shining shoes at the Handsome Barber Shop on Walnut Street, the main drag in my ghetto. That job paid about six dollars a week, a lot of money to a twelve-year-old boy with a limited view of what was possible. At the same time I was haunted by the thought that—barring some miracle I could not name—I might still be doing the same kind of work when I became a man.

Dear Adam,

The name of my miracle was football. In my judgment, you will need it, too. Not as a key to bettter possibilities, but just for the fun and the glory.

For me, in the 1940's, football was essential. The family *hui* had not yet been organized. So a college education was quite out of the question. My daddy and Aunt Letty simply didn't earn that kind of money.

By keeping my high-school grades well above the average and by working hard enough at football to win recognition on the All-City team, I won a scholarship from a club of former University of Wisconsin athletes who were interested in sending promising replacements to the football team.

Even with those credentials, however, I had trouble getting a tryout at Wisconsin. The university itself made few distinctions between black and white students—except in campus housing. But one man in the chain of command hadn't quite caught the spirit. He was the head football coach, Harry Stuhldreher. Harry had been the quarterback of the most celebrated backfield in football history, the Four Horsemen of Notre Dame. But one vital lesson of football had eluded him: Ability to carry the pigskin has nothing to do with pigmentation.

Luckily, a black Milwaukee lawyer, Jim Dorsey, who was a champion of all black families in my ghetto, knew a state senator named Robert Tehan. Senator Tehan pulled some strings—I don't know which ones—that got me onto the freshman team. Coach Stuhldreher never forgave me. But his career as a coach suddenly ended when his team lost too many games. The new coach, Ivy Williamson, regarded me as the best ball-carrier on the squad he inherited, and elevated me to the first team.

I am keenly aware that you are likely to doubt me when I say this—it sounds too much like the last page of a boys' novel—but, on my very first play from scrimmage under Coach Williamson, your daddy ran 49 yards through Navy for a touchdown. I went on to lead Wisconsin in scoring and ground-gaining that season, and wound up on the All-Big Ten team selected by the conference coaches. As it often happens with a black boy, however, even a triumph can produce complications.

The cheers I heard year after year in the football stadium, as well as the general nonracist climate on the campus, made it seem reasonable to me to tailor my academic courses to prepare me for newspaper work. No one except Stuhldreher had made an issue of my color. I didn't realize until very near graduation that nearly all newspapers in this country were controlled by Stuhldreher's spiritual cousins. There were no more than a half-dozen black reporters in the United States.

When I returned home to Milwaukee with a Bachelor of Science degree in journalism, my daddy was certain that I would come to my senses and give up that dream. He thought he had saved the day by making a verbal agreement with Gene Ronzani, head coach of the Green Bay Packers, that committed me, without my knowledge, to signing a contract with the team. The Packers were one of four professional football clubs ready to give me a tryout. But I had invested too much of myself in my dream to give up without a fight. And, alas, I did have to fight— with my daddy.

"Are you crazy?" he shouted. "The Packers are ready to pay you five thousand seven hundred dollars a season. That's as much as I make all year."

"I hate to disappoint you, Dad," I said. "But that's not what I want to do with my life."

"What newspaper is gonna give you a job?" he yelled. "Just name me one black man working on one of those big papers."

"Carl Rowan," I answered. *The Minneapolis Star-Tribune.*"

My daddy was surprised but not undone. "All right," he said with confidence. "Name me two."

He had me. Although I knew that a few other black men had made the breakthrough, I could not recall another name.

I persisted in my stubbornness, however. Which led to a fist fight. My daddy won, but both of us lost. I left his house after telling him that he was not my daddy anymore.

The very next day, I was hired as a sports writer by *The Milwaukee Journal*—mainly because of football. But nearly four years were to pass before my father and I grew up enough to stop being strangers to each other. By then, I had come to realize that my daddy was 99 percent right. The odds against a black man's getting the kind of job I got in the summer of 1950 was something like a thousand to one.

Chances are, my son, you will not have to tell a sad story to a lawyer or a state senator to get a college football uniform in the 1980's. Things are changing. Right now, in 1967, even southern universities occasionally put mixed teams on the field.

Nor will you cause eyebrows to rise—except mine perhaps—if you elect a course of study designed to prepare you for the Vice Presidency of the United States. I don't mean that I have any such hopes. I am simply saying that Mister Charlie occasionally allows one or two black men to go as far as they can. In your lifetime, political circumstances may lead a white Presidential candidate to decide he could improve his chances if he balanced his ticket with a black man. One who could pull a lot of votes.

No matter that the move may be merely cynical, it gives me satisfaction to be able to say to you, my son, as my daddy could never have said to me:

"My boy, someday you may grow up to be Vice President."

Dear Adam,

Another positive element in the America you will see in the 1980's and 1990's is a better attitude among black men about themselves. By then, the sense of racial shame that Mister Charlie has been teaching us for centuries will be almost totally replaced by racial pride.

You and your generation will not have to live through a single day of the self-torment of many black folk who accepted, even if unconsciously, white society's low assessment of the black race. Your daddy's generation was among the first to outgrow it.

For us, I think, it began after World War II, when African colonies began emerging as independent black states after centuries of white domination. In some cases, they had to shed their blood. And maybe there is a lesson in that. We began meeting black Africans as they visited and studied in this country. We were flabbergasted. These were black men, all right. But they clearly possessed a sense of pride in themselves, their tribe and their countries. Among their deepest concerns were completely nonracial ideas, like improving farm production, building more factories and schools, developing their own talents in order to serve the needs of their nations better. They were nothing at all like us or like the barefoot savages we had come to feel ashamed of in Hollywood movies about Tarzan, Jungle Jim and other Great White Hunters. In fact, there was something in their untroubled eyes that said: "Call *me* Bwana!" They hinted at our potential.

Gradually, the courage and self-assertion of our distant

cousins from Africa helped us assert ourselves in our new-found boldness. Which led to protest movements, marches and demonstrations. And when Mister Charlie kept pretending that he didn't understand "what you people want," he often found himself in the middle of a full-scale riot.

I told you in one of my first letters that there is a new expression of pride, self-confidence and militancy in the eyes of young black men who were born in the last thirty years. It is not a pose. They truly believe in their worth as human beings.

They are even voicing feelings that my generation would have found difficult to contemplate when we were in our teens.

I think I shall never forget the words of a nameless black boy in Newark—perhaps seventeen—who was interviewed on television shortly after one of the riots. I don't remember all that he said. But that's not important. There was one phrase that will live in my heart. He described his race as "the better half."

Dear Adam,

There's an old belief that each man has maybe two or three doubles somewhere in the world. Today I met one of yours. He is the leader of a street gang called the Black Cobras. Let's call him Raymond Cox.

I met Raymond and his teen-age gang at an antipoverty job-training center in the Bronx. A program called Operation Upward Bound. This was supposed to be one of my regular talks to encourage black boys to stay in school. But because Raymond looked so much like my idea of you at the age of sixteen and because he was so bitter, it turned out to be something of a two-man debate.

Before it began, I did manage to give them my views on "the secret of success," which most young people I address, black or white, seem eager to hear.

"If there is a secret to success, it might be an understanding of the fact that no one achieves success on his own. Everybody needs help along the way. The secret then is to develop attitudes that can make you the kind of person others are willing to help.

"That does not mean you have to be Superman. Or even Prince Charming.

"It does mean that you yourself have to be willing to give help to others. To accept responsibility. To carry out assignments from parents, teachers or anyone else in charge. Without being scolded or watched every step of the way. To show as much respect for other people as you expect to have shown to you."

"Bull!" A disgusted voice interrupted.

I made a pretense of searching several faces. Somehow, I knew it was the boy who looked like you. I had seen a challenge in his eyes from the moment I arrived. "I don't suppose the boy who made that crack is man enough to admit it," I said calmly. My face, I hoped, was expressionless.

Near the back of the room, Raymond jerked erect from a slump. "Ain't no chickens in my gang, mister," he said boldly. "I said bull and I meant it."

The rest of his gang was silent, watchful. Not one turned in his seat to look at their leader. Their eyes were fixed on mine. I sensed that the way I handled this challenge would determine how the entire afternoon would go.

"Am I supposed to guess what you meant by that?" I asked matter-of-factly.

"I'll save you the trouble," Raymond said. "We've already found out about respect, and it's nothing like what you said. If you want Whitey to respect you, you got to go up side his head, give him a bruise the first time he gets out of line."

No one else said a word. I saw their agreement, however, in subtle changes of facial expressions, the defiant looks in their eyes.

"Before I comment on your comment," I said—stalling to give another part of my brain a few seconds to come to my rescue—"I'd like to get one thing straight.

"I don't mind being questioned. I want all of you to feel free to question me about anything that doesn't sound right to you. But when you want to ask a question"—and here I fixed Raymond Cox with the most majestic eye I could muster—"you raise your hand. You don't just blurt out the first rude remark that comes to mind."

I didn't dare risk a pause to let that sink in. My brain had been busy, but I did not have time to evaluate what was still forming in my mind. I had to keep talking and hope that what came out would be good enough.

"Now about the question of giving and getting respect," I went on. "I know all about going up side Whitey's head for getting out of line. I went up side my share when I was a lot younger than I am now. They went up side my head more than a few times, too. But I finally realized that I wouldn't have time for anything else—that the rest of my life would simply drift—if I appointed myself to the job of beating up every white man who got out of line. It's a full-time job. There's no room for anything else."

Here I risked a pause. I could see in their faces that I was on the right track. Honesty *was* the best policy after all.

"Now it's my guess that none of you wants to devote your entire life trying to reform white folk with your fists. I think you're also interested in doing something with your lives—develop talents, raise families and so on. And if that's the case, you have an interest in what I've got to say. As difficult as it may be for you to accept it as wisdom now as members of a street gang, believe me there will come a time in your lives when each of you will also realize that what you're really fighting for isn't something that can be won in a rumble. More than that, you will come to realize that in spite of all the bruises you inflict, you don't really change anything. You can only change things by being better than the things you hate."

I paused again, sensing that I had recovered from Raymond's challenge.

"Now going back to the point I was trying to make

earlier—I hadn't finished with the attitudes I think you have to develop in trying to achieve success.

"You also have to keep your word. And never give it if there is any reason to believe that you might be forced to break it. You have to admit your mistakes—rather than try to shift the blame—and learn as much as you can from the experience.

"You've got to have the courage to stand alone against the crowd when you feel deep inside that you are right. Even if they call you chicken. You have to avoid making life more difficult for any other person. You have to tell the truth.

"If you develop those attitudes you are a successful human being. This doesn't guarantee success in terms of money and position, but—"

Raymond, slumped in his chair near the back of the room, held up his hand. I stopped.

"Is there a question back there?" I asked.

"Yeah," he said. "Sound to me like you talking about white boys. All that stuff don't mean nothing when you go to get a job, and the man sees you're black. It don't mean nothing to white folks what you like on the inside. It's what they see on the outside that counts, and on the outside you're black."

There was a general uproar of approval from his gang, about twenty black boys in all.

"I was coming to that point," I said, "and the point is this: The things I told you about becoming a successful human being apply to both blacks and whites. I was going on to say that black boys have to learn a couple of other things beyond what white boys learn—"

"We already know a couple of things they don't know," Raymond said loudly. His gang laughed even louder.

"All right," I said. "Suppose we let you take it from here."

"That was a joke, mister, a joke," he said. "Go ahead. Don't let me shake you up."

More laughter. Raymond was encouraged to continue.

"Maybe you could tell us if that's how you got to be such a big man. Being a successful human being and all that jazz. Or did you just brown-nose Mister Charlie?"

The room was silent now. The gang was watching me carefully to see whether I was getting angry enough to let this develop into a fight. I took a deep breath, but was surprised to find that I wasn't angry at all. Raymond looked too much like you, my son, for me even to think of trying to hurt him.

"All right," I said. "Let's talk about me for a moment. I think I can make the point I was about to make in another way.

"I can remember applying for at least fifty jobs when I first came to New York City about twelve years ago. I had about four hundred dollars in my pocket and a scrapbook full of my by-lines from my hometown paper in Milwaukee. I was turned down at least fifty times. Never mind the reasons. Being black, I knew in advance that I would not hear the real reason at a lot of places. Just double talk. But I also knew in advance that I couldn't let myself give up just because white men were giving me the business instead of giving me a job. That's the point I've been trying to make here today. A black boy has to learn that he can't afford to give up just because they make it tougher for him to make it than white boys. You have to make up your mind that you're going to try and keep on trying until you've won something. I know it's rough. And a lot of black boys have let it get them down. They throw up both

101

hands and say, 'Hell, what's the use of trying?' I know of others who find it easier to give up and blame their misfortunes on discrimination. In fact, they blame everything on discrimination. But I say a black boy can't afford to hide like that. Sure, there's a helluva lot of discrimination. But sitting back and feeling sorry for yourself won't help you one damn bit. If you're black, you've simply got to make an extra effort. And another extra effort. That's all there is to it.

"As I said, I was turned down fifty times when I went looking for a job in this city. But I filed my fifty-first application at *The New York Times*. The assistant managing editor who interviewed me was more interested in what I had done than in what color I was. They called me two weeks later. And I worked there six and a half years until I decided to go into broadcasting.

"Almost any black man that you might regard as successful can tell a story like mine. Black men will be telling stories like that for maybe a hundred years more. What you have to remember is that the stories show you what can happen if you make that extra effort. It shouldn't be that way, I know. It's not fair. But I'm just telling it like it is.

"And one day each of you in this room might have the same kind of story to tell. But only if you fully realize that to give up because the odds are against you is to help Mister Charlie keep you trapped in the hole. Where he claims you belong in the first place.

"You can't let him have the last laugh."

There was a long moment of silence in the room. Then the Black Cobras began applauding. What pleased me most was that Raymond Cox had started it.

Dear Son,

The office where I work became a battleground again today for one of my bloodless little wars with Mister Charlie. Only this time it was more like guerilla warfare. And Mister Charlie was a Miss. Let's call her Beverly White.

Beverly is a miniskirted redhead whose low-cut blouses and pink thighs have cost the company about one hundred man-hours a day in lost production since she joined our staff two months ago. The consensus is that hers is the kind of body that would be awarded to you as your secretary if you became chairman of the board. So far so good, except that Beverly has had a habit of surrounding me with words and looks that say: "I'm on your side so let's you and me have a good cry about it here and now."

Since the big news story today was another of those thinly disguised filibusters in the Senate to block a piece of black rights legislation, I knew I could expect to be exposed to Beverly White's assets. But the price was far too high. I would have to watch her threaten to cry, and listen to her familiar opinions of "those dirty old men from the South." Typical of her weepy species, she could somehow manage to reduce bigotry to a personal peeve. As if racists were a breed of insects that specialized in ruining picnics.

About twenty minutes after I had sat down at my typewriter, a shadow fell across my desk. I glanced up from the reams of wire-service copy I was sorting. And sure as God created firm nipples, there was Beverly White. On the verge of sobbing.

"It must be awful for you," she began, "having to

103

broadcast what those nasty old southerners are doing in the Senate. But I want you to know that I for one think they're terrible. Just terrible. How can they be so . . . so uncooperative?"

I assured Beverly that I had broadcast news stories like that in the past, and chances were I would broadcast others just like it.

"But that's just my point," she blurted, closer to tears than ever. "Why should they put you through that all the time? It's not fair."

She was telling me.

"I mean it's a very mean thing to do," she added.

Experience told me that unless I could think of a reasonable excuse to leave the newsroom, she would move on to her second favorite theme: What-do-you-think-we-as-intelligent-adults-on-the-race-question-can-do-about-it?

I wanted no part of that. It was a less than useless exercise.

"Beverly," I said. "I've been trying to give you a hint, politely, all these weeks that conversations like this bore me."

She blinked, surprised to the point of shock. A shadow of hurt flickered across her brimming eyes. "But I'm on your side," she protested. "What's wrong with that?"

"Nothing at all," I replied. "But I have it in my mind that the two of us put together don't have enough words or tears to change anything even a little bit. So why not save those tears for something practical?"

"Well, I feel it's up to those of us who—" She was framing an apology, but I cut her short this time.

"Let's put it this way, Miss White." I stared deliberately at the tantalizing crevice between the assets that peeked above the top of her blouse. "You've got a blouse-ful there and the right kind of legs to go with it. I'm sure you appreciate the attention they receive—from a safe distance. I'm also sure that you would not appreciate it if I limited my conversations with you to what you think we as intelligent adults on the sex question ought to do about it."

Beverly blushed. She also left me alone. She may not be beyond redemption.

It didn't take much more to reach another Charlie at the office not long ago.

"Your old desk was falling apart, so we junked it," an executive-type Charlie said to me. His voice was cheerfully apologetic. "The new one will be delivered tomorrow," he added, "and we'll set it up in that corner."

I thanked the man. He walked away. I really did need a new desk. And I didn't care where it might sit. That corner seemed all right to me.

Then a lesser-executive-type Charlie sidled up, having overheard the conversation. He was decent enough for the most part except for two annoying habits. He grinned relentlessly, and, lately, because the Black Revolution was so much in the news, he felt compelled upon seeing me to color any conversation with maybe the nastiest color in the world—murky white liberalism.

"What that desk business means," he muttered confidentially, "is that you'll get a seat; but it's going to be in the back of the bus."

He was clearly proud of what he thought was a joke. His grin was wider than ever.

I responded loudly and distinctly, "Shit!"

The world was too much with me that day, I guess.

"Jesus Christ," he said, taken aback. "What's the matter? I was only kidding."

It had been worth my loss of composure—which I never like to lose around Charlie—to see that grin disappear.

"I know you were kidding," I said very slowly, a habit when trying to hold down rage. "That is precisely the trouble. For the past week, you've been telling what amounts to the same stupid joke. But only to me. As I see it, if you and I are working together in the communications industry and if all you can talk to me about is race, then I say: Fuck it. You have absolutely nothing to communicate."

He muttered an apology, dropped his gaze to his shoe tops, and walked away.

The world was not changed, I know. But since then that particular Charlie has reformed, at least where your daddy is concerned. I like to think that there is one more Charlie in the world now who has learned that it is possible for a white man to talk with a black man day after day without referring to the color of their skins, that a black man would rather not be approached as nothing other than black. Aside from being patronizing and insulting, it limits the possibility of an exchange.

What I was trying to tell both those Charlies was that I am not some special enigma to be approached through an elaborate verbal minuet just because I am black, that I want to be approached simply and directly—just like any other man.

Dear Adam,

The fallout from the poisonous cloud of racism that hovers over this country can infect every square inch of a black man's life. And not just in his dealings with white men.

A few weeks ago, your daddy promised the black director of a ghetto youth center to come up and give my talk to his boys. Let's call the director Harry Day. We had never met face to face, but Harry was well known to every newsman in town after a stormy career as a full-time civil rights picket. Now—Harry explained on the phone—he had given up on demonstrations. He was instead trying to guide black boys out of the crippling despair that was settling over their lives—he called it "the ghetto mentality."

"I hate to admit it," he told me, "but I'm caught up in the same thing myself. I've given up on freedom in my time. I must've walked thirty thousand miles with a picket sign in the last three years, and look at where we are today. Like nowhere. Hell, you can't shake Whitey up unless you use a Molotov cocktail or a gun. I just can't see myself doing that. So all I got left to hope on is the kids. But they won't make it neither unless we get inside their heads and move them to where they start believing they got some kind of a chance."

When I arrived this afternoon in Harry's neighborhood, I found it dreary, dirty and depressing. Like ghettos around the world. His youth center was a dingy brick building, four stories tall, in the middle of a long block lined on both sides by almost identical buildings barely resisting the urge to crumble. There were rusty cans over-flowing with garbage along the curbs. Trash piles littered the sidewalks—mostly broken discarded furniture. Dozens of yammering black youngsters with old faces played in the trash piles or between them on the sidewalks. The stench from the garbage was unbearable. I was reminded of a story about Adolf Hitler walking through a concentration camp on an inspection tour. Hitler turned up his nose and said, "Jews stink." What he sniffed, of course, was Nazism.

Inside Harry's youth center, I was surprised. Everything was neat, clean and freshly painted in white trimmed with green—tables, chairs, bookshelves, everything. I could hear the uproar of manly teen-age voices coming from the upper floors. I found Harry sitting at an ancient roll-top desk in a cramped cubicle on the ground floor.

"Hey, man," he greeted me with a grin, extending his right hand. "Like welcome. Glad you got here so early."

We shook hands. Harry waved me into his chair—there was no room for another—and perched on the edge of the desk. He looked much younger than he had seemed on tele-vision. Perhaps thirty. Tall, dark and likable.

"I told the boys they could meet us in the rec room on the top floor at three-thirty," Harry said. "That means we got about fifteen minutes. Now I've read a lot about you, and I know you got a thing about talking to kids in the ghettos. Like I got my bag, and this is yours. But I want you to do something a little different today. A special favor."

"Like, man, you name it," I said. It was catching.

He rewarded me with a grin. "Well, let me explain something first. You have to understand that the kids living in this hell-hole ain't like a lot of other kids you've seen. This is Endsville, man, Endsville. They been left out of everything, and they know it. Only reason they listen to me at all when I tell 'em to stay out of trouble is they know I'm one of them. Just older. Like I was a high school dropout. You dig? I've done time. I ain't been able to make it.

"Now we come to you. These kids, they look at a guy like you—it's like you're somebody from outer space. You dig?"

"Not quite," I said, wondering what Harry was driving at.

"Well, here's the thing. You and me, we amount to about half the joker what could get through to these kids all the way. Wouldn't do no good for me to talk to 'em about staying in school and doing good deeds and all. Like they'd bust out laughing in my face. Okay. So we fudge a little. When you talk to 'em, you mess up your background a little. Don't make it sound so easy like it sounds in the stuff I read about you. Just say like you dropped out of school for a while. You got in trouble with the cops. Maybe you did a little time in reform school. Then you wised up; you straightened out, and you made it. You see what I mean? You made it with a second chance."

I saw.

"You mean you want me to lie for a good cause."

Harry shook his head, disgusted.

"Man, that ain't the way to look at it. Like we're talking about kids, man. Kids. We do it for the kids."

I didn't say anything for several seconds. I was a little stunned. The words I had planned to say to those kids were in my mind—accept responsibility, respect other peo-

ple, keep your word. I would have choked on the words
Harry wanted me to say.

When I tried, inadequately, to explain to Harry, he lost
his temper.

"Don't hand me that Sunday school crap," he said
fiercely. "Like this is the *real* world. You sound just like
Whitey. Maybe you learned to be too much like Whitey to
give us any help here."

I said I was sorry. Then I picked up my hat and left.

Driving home, I found it difficult to blame Harry Day.
It was that damned, lousy fallout again. What he had
asked me to do made me feel guilty and embarrassed.
Guilty because I had spent my life grabbing first chances.
Afraid, like Harry's boys, that there wouldn't be any second. Embarrassed because what he had said made mad
sense in a society that conspired to keep black boys in that
ghetto. I could not look into those young-old black faces
and tell them more lies.

Dear Adam-Smasher,

Just a few hours ago, as often before, I was enchanted by those special recognition signals you seem to reserve for your daddy.

As I came through the front door this evening, you were perched on the Tall Lady's lap. You quickly scrambled down to the floor, chirping and laughing, to make your way step by toddling step to me. The expression in your shining eyes was worth at least six million dollars. It said: "My daddy is my favorite giant; he is trustworthy, kind, wise and all-powerful—the kind of man I want to be."

By now, as you read this—a ripe old man in your teens —you are bound to have a less impressive picture. And it is likely to be tinted, I suppose, by what you will have heard about what kind of man I am. I wonder which of the things your daddy has already been called you may believe:

An atheist. A black snob. A nonmilitant pioneer. A subversive black power advocate. A talented news reporter. A white nigger. A fugitive from the ghetto. A black bard. A prude. An easygoing chap. A madman. A popular television personality. A fat cat. A scoundrel. The first Negro who did this or that. A hunky lover.

It is not my purpose here to deny any of those. Objectively, I suppose, I have been all those things here and there, in the eyes of one man or another.

I will confess that one of those terms—and only one— sets my teeth on edge: "The first Negro who . . ."

It is just about the insult supreme, completely negating

111

me as an individual while reducing the substance of my life to a statistic.

Mister Charlie never follows the phrase "first Negro who" with any kind of appraisal, good or bad, of personal capabilities. As if to say that the achievement is only relative. Not to be equated with that of whites.

One of my great ambitions is to pull off a minor triumph that somehow forces Mister Charlie into mouthing something like: "We the white majority should congratulate ourselves. We have just allowed another black man—the 659th—to scratch and claw his way through one of the most sacred closed doors in our society—door number 2,338."

Dear Adam,

Your adopted Uncle Julian has a phrase that gets right to one of the roots of your daddy's derangement: "The bastards won't let you live."

The bastards in this case, of course, have white skins and one-track minds—a kind of tunnel vision that makes it impossible for them to see the *you* that lives, learns, works and dreams inside your dark brown skin. In their view, almost anything you achieve results not from your own ability and your own sweat, but rather from an act of kindness by liberal elements in their society willing to make generous allowances for the stupidity and ineptness that comes with not being white.

At the same time, these particular bastards also refuse to let you fail at anything through your own shortcomings. They explain away your personal failures as a result of racial discrimination or of some racial flaw bred into your bones. In other words, they won't give you credit for the sunshine in your life, and they are much too understanding to blame you for the rain.

I'm telling you all this, Adam-Smasher, as a warning not to rely on white folks for an objective evaluation of yourself in any respect.

Many years ago, for example, when your daddy was a young tomcat barely out of college, I had a classic experience at one of those friendly interracial parties. It took place in a castle-like mansion in the white suburban fringe surrounding Milwaukee. Early that evening at the party,

I met a golden blonde dream—let's call her Paula Hotchkiss.

During the introductions, she learned that I was a by-line reporter for the largest newspaper in the state of Wisconsin, *The Milwaukee Journal*. Paula's big blue eyes grew bigger. "How marvelous," she said in awe. "I confess that I've never noticed your by-line in *The Journal*. But from now on I'll make it a point to look for it." Her smile was positively dazzling.

I had met her kind before, of course. Their attitude reminds me of the old story about the dog that could walk on his hind legs. The remarkable thing was not that he did it well, but that he could do it at all.

Anyway, quiet dance music was playing on the hi-fi set, and, although I was a terrible dancer in those days, I swept Paula Hotchkiss into my arms. Oops! I stepped on her foot. We stopped, laughed and tried again. This time she stepped on my foot. We made about five false starts like that. Paula was game, determined. She was one of those cartoons you see in slick magazines of the wealthy young things turned out every year by Radcliffe College—sincere, direct and liberal-minded, with a full-steam-ahead approach to life. Also, she had a strong tendency to lead her partner on the dance floor instead of following slavishly like those elegant young things turned out by Vassar.

After the fifth false start, Paula Hotchkiss gave up. She took a step backward, looked me straight in the eye and said quite seriously but without criticism: "Your trouble is you've got too much rhythm in your body. But then, you can't help that, can you? It's what you were born with— I mean it's a part of your African background and all."

"I don't know," I said. "When I step on a Negro girl's

foot, I'm usually told I'm a lousy dancer. I guess maybe I am. But I'm great at sitting-the-next-one-out."

We sat out quite a few. And later—after some furtive necking in the kitchen—we wound up alone together in a guest bedroom upstairs. A few other couples were similarly occupied in other rooms, having also sneaked away from the party.

As soon as she stepped out of her underthings, Paula threw her arms around my neck. Her voice was intimate, warm and husky in my ear. "You don't have to go easy with me," she whispered. "I understand about the things that make Negro men so much better—the way you tear into a woman like an animal."

Well. Another one of those. As a matter of fact, I was feeling a little unsure of myself at that moment, and my experience in the boudoir at that stage of my life was not impressively extensive. I had just then been trying to re-member all the advice my daddy gave me about women several years earlier. Always be gentle, he had told me. Make her feel you care about her as well as what's between her legs. Build her up slowly for it. And always make sure she gets hers the first time around, even if you have to hold back yourself. That way she'll be glad to come back any time.

Frankly, I would like to tell you that I abandoned Paula Hotchkiss then and there—that I put on my pants and walked out nobly, tossing a lofty sentiment over my shoulder. Like, "Madam, as a gentleman I can only say this affair is off."

But that would be a lie.

The truth is I had not very often had access to the kind of blonde forbidden fruit she represented. And I was hungry for it—caught up in the same mystique. So what I said, I'm afraid, was, "Maybe you'd better tell me just how rough you want it."

Her tongue darted into my ear. Then she bit the lobe. "Let's pretend," she said, "that this is a rape."

As it turned out, all I had to do was penetrate Paula's pubic hair. Almost immediately, her body stiffened; she clawed my back with her fingernails, moaned and quivered violently. It was all over just as I was getting started. Her vivid imagination had been much more potent than any expertise at my command.

———

P.S.——Another example of how "the bastards won't let you live" involved my first trip to a national political convention a few years ago. My second year in television. The Republican Party gathered in San Francisco to nominate a Presidential candidate. During the course of that three-day convention, a great deal of the live TV coverage was concerned with keeping track of the Republican leaders between sessions of formal business at the San Francisco Cow Palace.

I was stationed with my television remote unit in the lobby of the Mark Hopkins Hotel. Our competitors from the rival networks were there too. It was a key location since the leading contender for the G.O.P. nomination that year, Senator Barry Goldwater, was in a suite on one of the upper floors. Which meant that almost everybody who was anybody in Republican politics had to come and go past our cameras and microphones. The traffic was heavy. But the lobby was also a tough location for TV work. It was jammed all day long with party workers, curious onlookers, newspaper photographers, radio reporters, the police and secret service men and film crews from California TV stations. And the steel platforms supporting the live TV cameras high above the crowd also took up space and made it difficult to move around. It was virtually impossible, in fact, if you had to drag your mike cables behind you.

But luck was with me, and no one else. The engineers in my gang rigged a wireless mike with a small battery to fit in my pocket. There were no trailing cables, which meant more personal mobility. I could weave and shoulder my way through the crushes. As a result, we beat the pants off the competition time and again. Sometimes the other reporters, chained to their cables, never even reached the scene of the interview. At other times they arrived late to join me in the questioning.

That was precisely the situation in the Mark Hopkins lobby on the final night of the convention. Senator Goldwater was returning to the hotel in triumph, surrounded by bodyguards, aides and well-wishers. He had won the nomination. Upon seeing me again as I shoved a microphone under his chin for the umpteenth time that week, he grinned and said: "You've been doing a great job here. You always manage to get through when the others can't. That's very good."

"Thank you, Senator," I said. "Thank you very much."

His compliment and my response were heard from coast to coast.

In the days that followed the convention, some newspapers and many of my white liberal friends commented on Goldwater's public compliment. But strangely, none of their remarks dealt in any way with the substance of what the man had said about my work. The comment from your adopted white Uncle Bruce was typical: "Goldwater was just making a subtle pitch for the Negro vote in November."

———

P.P.S.——The third phase of how "the bastards won't let you live" is, to my mind, even more depressing than the ones I described above. It further denies a black man any claim to merit as an individual.

You will find, for instance, that some white folks will give you a rave notice for even the tiniest ability you might show. That's because they don't expect as much from you —beyond the boudoir, that is—as they expect from men of their race.

And if you happen to be a scientific genius, they don't see you as a genius. What they see is an "exceptional Negro." I'll have more to say about that later.

So as I said earlier, it would be a waste of time to depend on your friendly neighborhood white liberal for an accurate judgment of what you're worth.

Dear Adam,

Several nights ago, I wrote you a letter about the ways people have described your daddy. Well, today at the office, a liberal-type Mister Charlie spat a new one in my face—"a sensible Negro."

Like everyone else these days, we were discussing the violent aspects of the Black Revolution, the periodic riots in the ghettos. He wanted to know why "a sensible Negro like you doesn't try to use his influence to calm things down in Brooklyn."

Could a truly sensible Negro ever bring himself to that?

As the late Malcolm X often told us: "You get your freedom by letting your enemy know that you'll do anything to get your freedom. Then you'll get it. It's the only way you'll get it."

I'm afraid that your daddy didn't handle himself too well in that conversation. Don't ask me why. I simply told him that the black people in the Brooklyn ghetto were angry, and for valid reasons; that they probably wouldn't listen to anyone, least of all to someone they could regard as a fat cat; that they would be all too aware that I make more money in television broadcasting in one year than most of them would see in a lifetime.

What I should have told him—what I failed to say like a man—was that I am secretly pleased about the riots, that I'm a bona fide riot fan, that nothing would please the tortured man inside me more than seeing bigger and better riots every day. Not because I believe in violence. But be-

119

cause black violence seems the only form of protest that engages Mister Charlie's attention.

I also failed to say that whenever I watch a film replay of a riot on television, I root for the blacks—even though I know how the battle turns out. Like Mister Charlie when he watches the *Late Late Shows*, and roots for General Custer against the Indians.

Dear Adam,

While the two of us were taking a few turns around our block this afternoon—you in your stroller—we stopped for a few minutes in our friendly neighborhood drugstore. The Tall Lady had asked me to buy some vitamins. Our friendly neighborhood pharmacist volunteered the observation that you seemed to be small for your age. My response, I'm afraid, was in the range that nuclear scientists call overkill.

"If you think I'm going to apologize for *anything* about this kid," I snapped, "you're out of your goddamn mind."

Luckily, our friendly neighborhood pharmacist was also a father, a diplomat and a gentleman. He did not escalate the conflict.

Later, it occurred to me that my behavior in the drugstore was perhaps symptomatic of what is described as tunnel vision—a special viewpoint dictated by a particular circumstance; in this case, the circumstance of being a proud father. I was reminded of a friend, a vice-squad detective, who is overly suspicious of every man he meets.

I view the world through another tunnel even larger. The disenchanted tunnel at my end of the picture tube, from which I look out at the news six days a week.

The news this week has reinforced my discouragement about the American political scene.

Almost everybody in Washington—Democrats and Republicans—agrees that there is a real need for a tax increase to help pay for the Vietnam war; to continue and expand domestic programs such as creating more jobs for

121

the poor; to hold down inflation and reduce the government's debts. But nobody wants to be associated with a tax rise in the minds of voters. So each party is working hardest at blaming the other for the economic crisis that brought the need for more taxes. Little is being done about the problem itself.

At the same time, Republican congressmen are demanding that the Democratic President cut government spending by billions; that is, cut back on programs to help those segments of the population who need help in the worst way. Nobody wants to be associated with that in the minds of voters either. So the President is insisting that Congress make the cuts. And take the blame.

In other words, all of these public servants, sworn to promote the general welfare, are more concerned about their chances in the next election than about doing what they believe needs to be done in the interests of the people they are supposed to serve.

Dear Adam-Smasher,

Fortunately, my son, your daddy is not too old to learn. The Tall Lady helped prove it today.

While watching us play my favorite game—taking turns handing off your tot-size rubber football to each other—she made this observation:

"It seems to me that you're so busy teaching Adam the right way to handle that thing, you're forgetting to let him in on the fact that football is a game, that it's supposed to be a lot of fun."

Her point was well taken. I had been looking through another tunnel. I began correcting my mistake. At the same time, curiously, her point reminded me—now don't laugh —of sex. I have written some letters to you on that subject, but usually to clarify something else. Perhaps I should include a word about sex itself.

And I will in my very next letter. But first—as we say in television—this message: One more story about the sex preoccupation to document another worthwhile point.

Several years ago when your daddy was something of a big-time newspaper reporter, I was sent to Chicago to cover a week-long political happening. Dozens of other big names were also in town for the same story. And when not busy running down the news or making with the clickety-clack-clack on our typewriters, we spent our free time eating, drinking and seeing the sights together.

Well, one evening the clique of seven I traveled with— all white except your daddy—was having dinner in the dining room of our hotel. Our acknowledged leader was a

123

giant in our profession, a rather arrogant man in his early thirties, about three years older than I was at the time. I shall call him Perry Kind.

Perry told the rest of us that a local businessmen's club had arranged a stag party for certain visiting dignitaries and certain members of the press. The varsity, he said. Our seven-man clique was among the chosen few.

"Just between me and you, fellows," said Perry, "I have it on the highest authority, as we say in the profession, that they've brought in a good-looking bunch of playgirls for our convenience. And best of all, gang, the club that's inviting us is picking up the tab. We get the whole works—lots of booze, a nude floorshow and willing girls—all for free."

During the general hubbub of approval that rose up over our table, I thought I spotted a guilty look in the eyes of one or two. It was easy to guess why: Every last one of us was married. But nobody said a word about that.

Later, as we were leaving the dining room—laughing and bantering as men on their way to forbidden delights always do—I quietly made a detour in the hotel lobby. I had taken perhaps five steps in the opposite direction from the rest when Perry Kind noticed my defection.

"Hey, come on," he said pleasantly. "You gotta stay with the gang, old man."

I smiled and shook my head.

Perry raised both eyebrows and played his ace. "I personally guarantee that there will be enough blondes to go around."

The rest were silent, noncommital. But clearly anxious to witness this.

"Well, the fact is, Perry," I said matter-of-factly, "I'm

not going. I didn't want to say anything since each man
has to decide what he thinks is fun. This party you're going
to—well, it's just not my way."

Perry became indignant. He questioned my intelligence,
my manners and my manhood.

I said I was a married man.

No one else said a word.

Finally, Perry said angrily, "If you don't go with us,
I'll lose a lot of my respect for you."

Until that moment I really had been wavering a bit.

"If the only way I can win your respect is to cheat on
my wife," I said, "then what the hell, Perry. I frankly
don't want your respect."

Perry Kind had no comeback for that. Around us there
were sheepish grins and sighs of relief, barely audible.
Without a word, the clique broke up into seven individual
men. Not one went to the party.

Dear Adam,

Now about that letter on sex itself.

Experience has taught your daddy that perhaps the most wonderful thing about being in bed with a loving woman is the way it lifts my spirits; the way it isolates me from all else in this world, leaving a pure sensation of pleasure.

And how are these miracles achieved?

Well, let me explain it like this: With love and respect between them, a man and a woman will soon find their own perfection.

Of course, there are taboos forbidding what your daddy regards in many instances as noble experiments. Fortunately, however, many taboos may safely be dismissed. In the first place, the people most concerned about such restrictions are one of three undesirable things:

Sincere fools who accept the taboos, and deny themselves.

Hypocrites who urge taboos upon others to expunge feelings of guilt about what they themselves enjoy.

And celibates—such as hermits, priests and nuns—whose vows forbid sex on any terms.

There was a story about celibates in one of my newscasts a few weeks ago. Some thirty Roman Catholic monks resigned from a monastery in Mexico after a few private talks with a psychiatrist. They had learned about themselves. Some said they finally realized that they had joined the sexless branch of Christianity not because of deep religious convictions. But because they had unreasonable fears about making love with a woman.

As far as I'm concerned, if anyone expects me to accept his rules on sex, he must prove that he doesn't have dusty cobwebs inside his skull or in his crotch.

Having said all that, I can almost hear your next question: Is there any place where daddy does draw the line?

Great hounds in the harem! I am not peddling perversion.

For those of us who are gentlemen there is a rule—just one: Give pleasure only, never pain.

Dear Adam-Smasher,

Now that you have learned a few football fundamentals, though barely seventeen months old, I have decided to discontinue our informal quarterback training program for a few years. I am confident you will remember what you have learned; and I don't want to overdo it. As some wise man once observed long ago, even virtue owes homage to proportion.

But just in case I don't get a chance to explain later when you are older, perhaps ready to play football, I should make it clear here and now that my hang-up on football is not as simplistic as it probably seems. Let me assure you that it is not limited to the desire, as the sports pages would put it, to see my son "follow the glory trail his father blazed on the gridiron."

It happens that football, as much as almost anything else in my life, had a great deal to do with my becoming the person I am. Which I rather like.

Football is a game of civilized violence; civilized in the sense that though physical injury is possible, injury is not the object of the game. Unlike the barbaric sport called boxing, no points are given for hurting a man.

I found that football was a lot less violent at the bottom of a pile-up than it had seemed from the sidelines. And I began to learn on the field that whatever I might fear could often be a lot less frightening if I faced it. To me then, as a boy, football was something like the terror that some primitive African tribes call "The Tiger"; sooner or later every man must face one, and the sooner the better.

The football field taught me a kind of self-discipline to keep going though weary and faced with awesome odds.

Also, to be more than gracious in victory and less than undone by defeat.

It all added up, I suppose, to a kind of self-confidence, still with me. And that this society makes demigods of its football heroes helped me to break the cycle of poverty that had trapped my daddy as his daddy had been trapped before him. Even Mister Charlie cheers when his favorite team scores a touchdown, regardless of the ball-carrier's color.

One unforeseen consequence of football occurred when I returned to Milwaukee after having been graduated from the university. A sizable black delegation representing the Democratic Party power structure in the ghetto came to me one evening and begged me to run for political office. For the city council.

They were not dissuaded by my explanation that I knew next to nothing about being a city councilman, that I had not studied law in college, and that I had been away from Milwaukee so long, four years, that I was not really familiar with the city's problems.

"We understand all that," their spokesman told me. "But the fact is your football career has made you the most popular young man in town. You can win this election easy."

I gave them a flat No.

As you might imagine, that incident contributed to my distaste for politics. We are the sum total of all our anecdotes.

I am still quixotic and believe that being popular enough to win a job is not nearly so important as being competent enough to handle that job. No politician I have ever met —black or white—would go along with that theory. Most of them would sooner endorse this view:

First you win the election. Then you worry about what you can do in office to help your chances in the next one.

Your daddy's career as a conscientious dropout got a good boost from the city council episode. What finally shoved me out of society was the Doc Sperling affair.

About seven years ago I developed a sharp, relentless pain in my guts. I went to an elderly doctor—the nearest to our apartment—a general practitioner named Joel Sperling. He did not treat my guts. Just my mind.

After examining me thoroughly and making a number of chemical tests, Doc Sperling told me I was a model of physical health.

"It must be tension," he decided. "Spastic colitis. First cousin to an ulcer. What the devil are you worrying about, young man?"

I could scarcely believe that he was serious.

"What am I worrying about?" I blurted. "Doc—the bomb, the bigots, people starving—the whole lousy mess."

Old Doc Sperling looked me straight in the eye without blinking.

"I've got news for you, buster," he said evenly. "They ain't gonna ask you about it."

I could almost hear something shift in my brain. Doc Sperling had given me what proved to be the only tonic I needed. The pain in my guts disappeared within the hour. It has never returned for an instant.

All I can do, I decided, is to live my life in such a way as to not add to the troubles the human race already has. Probably, if every man would do so little, the world would have more laughter. Fewer tears.

Dear Adam,

This is Election Day, my son. The bars are closed. The polls are open. And the Tall Lady has left us alone. She has gone to cast her vote, against my better judgment, and you have settled down to an afternoon nap. Now I wish to explain why, as part of your daddy's madness, I would not vote if they paid me.

I do not share the white man's confidence in the democratic process at any level—voting, whether in clubs, Congress or courts. Because the question is never what is right, but what the greatest number says is right. And the greatest number is always white. They usually vote against me.

I realize that my position is perhaps unwise, and I am not necessarily recommending it. Your daddy, as they say in the ghettos, is simply telling it like it is.

My refusal to vote, in an age when black men are fighting and dying for the right to vote, is a slice of the black man's cake of ironies. But you see, by the time your daddy was old enough to vote, I had learned that in this country voting is a white man's charade. With its indirect as well as direct results.

It was by legislative voting that they gave us the runaway slave law, which allowed them to return my great-great-grandfather to his master.

It was also by voting that they deceived us with those so-called Civil Rights Acts that promise freedom now. These are nullified, it seems, by other votes on lower levels.

It was by voting on all levels that they came up with that inescapable maze of laws, codes, ordinances and gentlemen's agreements that deny black men more than accidental access to the fruits of the American dream.

It is by voting for judges who ignore justice, or voting for the hacks who appoint them, that they convict, jail and condemn my kinsmen, almost at whim, on the flimsy evidence of their blackness.

It is by the same kind of voting that they regularly excuse their own kind from the penalties legally due to them for denying and brutalizing my brothers.

And finally, it is by several kinds of voting that they interpret the Constitution to mean that it is perfectly natural and fair to run this society on the premise that black men are not quite equal and therefore should not be free.

So voting is not for me. It is too insulting and degrading to support Mister Charlie's pretenses, to pretend that I am fooled. I am proud to say that your daddy has never even stooped to register. My self-respect forbids me to accept as my due the crumbs of Mister Charlie's gaudy feast—the piddling fallout from his election charades.

He calls them "the democratic process in action." But no matter what promises he makes, regardless of what issues he and his kinsmen in the great majority—the power structures—may or may not decide to vote on and regardless of how the votes turn out, it all adds up to the same:

Voting is a wonderful civilized institution—if used with integrity, justice, fair play. It *can* move mountains, create better living and change the world. But somehow, in this climate, it doesn't work unless you are white.

Dear Adam,

The Tall Lady has just blistered my ears with a stern lecture, perhaps deserved, without raising her voice in the slightest. Her eyebrows, however, were practically scraping paint off the ceiling. Your daddy's crime was forgetting this afternoon what Dr. Spock's baby bible says about shouting when there is an infant in the house: Don't. Not even if that infant is a distance away, in his bedroom with his mother.

Let me assure you this instant that I wasn't shouting at you or the Tall Lady, but at a stranger. An almost innocent young woman with a pretty white face, sent here by *Newsweek* magazine.

Now that she has gone and the Tall Lady has kissed away your tears, I want to explain why your daddy forgot to speak like a gentleman.

The young woman from *Newsweek* had telephoned yesterday to ask for an interview. She had been assigned, she explained, to write a story about television personalities and their problems. I was on her editor's "must-get" list.

Well, between that phone call and the time she showed up this afternoon, I spent many of my free moments thinking of things I could tell that might be of unusual interest.

There was, for example, my making the switch from newspapers and magazines to television. Having to learn to write for the ear instead of the eye. And the way I crammed to learn about magnetic sound tracks. The subtleties of film editing. The flexibility gained by cut-aways.

The difference between double projection and double system. The mysteries of those scrambled electronic signals that make pictures on video tape. How to handle a live remote from a mobile unit in the field. The loss of privacy that goes with appearing in a million strange living rooms nightly. The demands the public makes on the few free hours that should be given to the family. Girls who develop crushes. The incredibly complicated teamwork of many technicians and assistants to put a good newscast together. The zany things that can and do go wrong in the studio.

And, of course, there were anecdotes to point up each of those.

That young lady was going to get one helluva good inside-television story.

However, when she arrived, ballpoint pen and pad at the ready, she politely refused my offer of a drink and quickly erased my illusions.

She was plainly flabbergasted when I suggested: "Maybe we should start with the basic problems. Learning to write for the ear instead of the eye, and getting used to a one-sided conversation with a camera."

"Oh dear, I didn't mean *that* kind of problem," she said. "What my editor wants me to get is the problems a *Negro* faces in television."

Great herrings in the hogwash! The same old tasteless slop.

I insist that I did not use a single four-letter word. But that is a mere technicality. The edge in my voice and its volume turned every single phrase into vilification.

"You've come to the wrong man," I said. I spat it out, I guess. "I don't play that stupid game." My words whetted my indignation, honed it into savage rage. "But off the record—I mean absolutely not for publication—I'll tell you the problem the Negro faces in television. It's the same problem he faces everywhere else in this lousy stupid country: The fact that 99 percent of the whites he comes up against think exactly like that stupid editor who sent you here with that stupid narrow-minded question. They can't think of an individual black man in terms of what makes him the particular man he happens to be, that he might have some special talent, that he might have something to contribute. All they see when they look at a black man is a problem."

She was chagrined, but sympathetic. It was her editor's idea, she assured me. "But could I please use what you've just told me?" She leaned forward on the edge of her chair, her ballpoint poised. "I mean without using your name or identifying you in any way?"

"Absolutely not," I spat. "Not a word."

There was a moment of silence, which let me hear you crying in the distance. I realized then how terrible my voice must have sounded. To everyone. I owed the young woman an apology.

"Forgive me, please," I said, much calmer now. I could still hear you wailing in the background. "I didn't mean to take it out on you. I know you're only doing what they told you. But it's a thing that bugs me more than I can make you understand. Like I'm tired of being approached as a black iceberg—with most of my real self submerged in a sea of white assumptions."

She smiled faintly. "I think I do understand," she said. "It's like the thing they're always doing about women. I get bugged by that myself."

135

Miss Newsweek folded her notebook and started slowly for the door.

"If you ever want to do a story about television," I said, "I'll be more than happy to give you all the help I can. But as for this story—well, just tell your editor that you gave it the old college try; that I flatly refused to play his stupid game."

"Thank you," she said. "I'll remember." She closed the door as gently as she could.

Dear Adam,

Mister Charlie has just surveyed public opinion in the black ghettos, I am told. From it, he learned that right now, late in 1967, the most popular figure in the Black Revolution is the Rev. Dr. Martin Luther King, Jr.

Although Mister Charlie hasn't said so, I suspect that is a great relief. He undoubtedly found comfort in the fact that the nonviolent Dr. King ranks Number One in the ghetto mind instead of H. Rap Brown, Stokely Carmichael, George Washington Ware, James Forman or the other black madmen of my time.

But it's a false comfort. It seems obvious to me that though most black men still go along with nonviolence, it does not mean that they are not as angry as H. Rap Brown; or that they are willing to wait indefinitely for the hunkies to come around. Instead, I think, they recognize individually something voiced not long ago by Roy Wilkins of the National Association for the Advancement of Colored People:

"Black people are not so stupid as to believe that they could win a war against the whites. Even forgetting the fact that we're nutnumbered ten to one. The whites control most of the guns, most of the money, and all of the tanks, planes and bombs, et cetera."

While I am talking about the popularity of captains in the Black Revolution, I should also point out that Mister Charlie's approach, the reasoning behind his poll in the ghetto, is not to be taken seriously. Habitually, he looks for "safe" Negro leaders. And he often creates them by

137

giving special public attention to whichever black captain seems least dangerous, the one who is willing to settle for the least.

Actually, there is no such animal as a Negro leader in Mister Charlie's sense; that is, there is no black man who can speak for all of his cousins, or even most of them. Just as there is no leader who can speak for all Jews, Italians, Lithuanians, Democrats or Republicans. There are Catholics who disagree with the Pope. Yet somehow Mister Charlie persists in the notion that black men are less inclined to think for themselves, ready to follow any black scarecrow who has been photographed with the frontmen in the power structure.

Black men, too, are individuals. We disagree among ourselves, as whites disagree about the things that affect their lives and what their so-called leaders say in public.

I have no idea what percentage of my black cousins would agree with my evaluation of the so-called Negro leaders. I respect and reject them all.

Dr. King, for example, I think of as a great man by any civilized standard. But I cannot and will not go along with his theory, taken from Mister Charlie's Bible, that black men should accept violence at the hands of whites and turn the other cheek. For more of the same. To me, that amounts to self-mutilation; perverting yourself into something much less than a man.

Neither can I go all the way with Rap Brown and the other reckless revolutionaries who say, "Let's burn this country down, hunkies and all." I am convinced that more violence, burning and rioting is strategically necessary—and I don't wish to stop it—to jar Mister Charlie out of his comfortable dream. But deep down I cling to the

138

notion that violence is wrong whether whites inflict it against blacks or vice versa.

I also have serious reservations about the approach taken not so long ago by Robert Carson of CORE, who is trying to establish an all-black community in the South. Carson argues that blacks must escape from this sick white society to avoid further contamination. He is right about the sickness. But to accept membership in an all-black society in this country would be the first step toward becoming the very thing black men say they hate in Mister Charlie.

I want to stress, however, that in spite of my reservations, I don't wish to see any of those approaches abandoned. It is my guess that these trials and errors may help convince Mister Charlie that he is never going to have peace of mind in this country on his terms alone, that desperate black men will always be trying first this wild scheme and then that one. Until the basic wrong has been righted.

Dear Adam-Smasher,

Those fifteen friendly strangers who threatened to smother you with affection this weekend have finally gone. What a relief! You will meet them again and again over the years, however. They are kinfolk—uncles, aunts and cousins on your daddy's side of the family. Since no children are brought to our annual reunions, always at this time of the year, they went overboard for you out of longing for their own youngsters hundreds of miles away in Wisconsin, Michigan, Illinois, Indiana and Tennessee.

I am confident you will recover from the siege. But the Tall Lady says you may be spoiled now, having been worshiped like an infant potentate for three full days. And the presents! The Tall Lady says no little boy needs that many toys. Some will go to boys who don't have fifteen doting relatives.

Why are children left out of our family reunions?

Mainly because the purpose of the gathering is to plan collectively what we can do for all the youngsters in our tribe: Money, advice, job contacts, special arrangements for projected trips and transfers of household items from a branch of the family that no longer needs them to the branch that needs them most. Your playpen and the clothes you have outgrown, for example, will soon be going to Tennessee.

This tradition began about twenty years ago at the insistence of that round-faced gray-haired woman who held you on her lap more than anyone else, Aunt Letty from Detroit. The acknowledged leader of our tribe. She is also my favorite aunt. As I've said before, when I was a boy about your age, it was Aunt Letty who looked after me—the way the Tall Lady takes care of your needs and whims.

Aunt Letty is sixty-two years old now, though she doesn't look it. She was our first college graduate, and it was her idea that every child in our tribe should be guaranteed a chance to go to college. She feels so strongly about college for black boys and girls that in her spare time she runs a free school in the Detroit ghetto where she lives by choice. To encourage black youngsters and help them with their studies.

"There are new opportunities opening up all the time," Aunt Letty is fond of saying. "But Confucius say opportunity empty if no one prepared to seize it."

Aunt Letty always speaks her mind. Confucius is her way of softening the impression that she is giving orders. None of us in the tribe is fooled, however. Aunt Letty gives the orders, all right. Her orders are always wise. And we obey the best we can. In the *hui*, or family assistance program that the old girl has organized us into, each one is committed to donating 10 percent of his annual income, after taxes. The money goes into a fund, administered by Aunt Letty. She spends as much as is necessary to send the tribe's children to college; she invests the rest as she sees fit, and the profits are added to the fund.

This weekend she announced when all of us were together that some would have to donate a bit more.

"Confucius say when cost of living go up, cost of college go into orbit."

After determining that the average income of the nine contributing branches of the family—eight couples and

141

herself—was $14,000, she explained that the extra assessment was necessary because two more youngsters in the tribe would be starting college next fall. Both in the Indiana branch. She peered over her rimless glasses—first at me, then at Uncle Mark and finally at Cousin Raymond. Uncle Mark is a lawyer in Nashville. Cousin Raymond is a commercial airline pilot who lives in Chicago. Our incomes are far above the family average.

"How much more does Confucius say we should contribute to the *hui* this time, Aunt Letty?" Cousin Raymond asked with a smile.

Aunt Letty smiled back and focused on him over her glasses. "Confucius say fifteen hundred too much, five hundred not enough, but one thousand each just right."

The three of us sighed, along with our wives. Then we wrote the checks.

Dear Adam,

On Sunday you watched your daddy moderate a public-affairs panel show on the local TV. By now, you might recognize these as conspiracies pitting three or four newsmen against a willing victim, a public figure. The Tall Lady told me you kept pointing to the screen in our living room and saying "Daddy, Daddy"—unconvinced that your daddy was not somehow imprisoned inside the box. You did not comment on the genteel bloodletting, she said. Nor on my performance. Alas!

My first experience with such a show is worth recounting to you because its friendly neighborhood villain is one of those self-deceived and deceptive white liberals that you will meet again and again.

They prey on the unsuspecting black man at the upper end of the socioeconomic scale—the black man who has made it. First, they approach you as if you were just another brain surgeon, engineer or astronaut. Then wham! They let you have it right between the eyes with a 100-caliber slug of bigotry, which they don't even know they have. Their purpose—or so it seems—is to keep you from getting uppity or even comfortable. You may be well educated, well mannered, well groomed, well heeled and well known, but they want to make sure you don't have the fancy notion that you are also well accepted. In other words, they hurt like hell.

It was about five years ago, when I was learning the business but had done well enough to be seen frequently on the air, on film and video tape. One day I got a long-distance call from an affiliated station in Washington. The man on the other end of the line—let's call him Barry Stump—was the moderator of a popular panel show. He said he had heard I was doing excellent work as a reporter for the New York station. Could I come to Washington the next weekend to be a panel member on his program?

"Barry, I'd love to," I said, flattered at being recognized as a pro by one of the established giants. I was also thinking about the fat fee I would get. "Who's to be the victim this week?"

"James Farmer," he answered, "the civil rights leader and national director of CORE."

Barry had sprung the trap.

However, since I had clearly established myself—at least in my own mind—as a general assignment newsman, I still was not sure. Hadn't Barry called me at least partly because of my proven ability—after twelve years with *The Milwaukee Journal* and *The New York Times* and some time in television—to ask brief and penetrating questions, gently but directly, to develop a news story on the spot?

So after only a moment of hesitation, I said, "Okay."

"But look, Barry," I added. "I have no objection to questioning James Farmer. I've done it many times on film here in New York. As a matter of fact, I know the guy very well. He and I live in the same apartment building. But I'm determined not to allow myself to be limited in this business to covering only Negro news. So since this is to be my very first appearance on your show, here's the deal I'd like to make. I'll appear on the program next Sunday and help get the story on Farmer. But I want your word now that you'll invite me back on your show—not

144

the next week or even next month necessarily, but very soon—to interview somebody not connected with the civil rights movement. Okay?"

Now it was Barry Stump's turn to hesitate.

"Gosh," he said uncertainly. "I can't guarantee that."

"Why not?" I asked.

This time Barry didn't hesitate at all.

"Well, what else do you know anything about?" He was not really challenging me. His tone said he couldn't believe I was serious.

I was finding it hard to believe his disbelief. In fact, I couldn't help laughing a little.

"Oh, come on, Barry," I said, half-joking. "Be serious. Don't tell me you think I can't read and do my homework for a given assignment—the same as you and any other reporter on that show?"

Barry Stump was not convinced.

"Well, I'll think about it," he said after another notable pause. "But for now, let's forget about your coming down for the program with Farmer this weekend. Maybe I'll call you again sometime."

He never did.

Dear Adam,

In trying to paint a portrait of Mister Charlie for you, I have neglected one of his more flattering characteristics. Underneath that white mask he is often a great deal like you and me—quite human.

I would estimate that in 15 percent of my face-to-face dealings with Mister Charlie, he impresses me as being just another individual. Who happens to be white, not a hunky.

I try to remember that 15 percent whenever I meet Mister Charlie. And until he says or does something that reflects the other 85 percent, I forget that he is a descendant of Simon Legree and perhaps a distant cousin of a modern-day Alabaman named George C. Wallace.

The 85 percent often shows up in subtle ways. For example, some of the whites I have worked with over the years felt free to tell me their most sacred secrets, things that should be told only to their psychiatrists. My guess is that they did so—and still do so—because deep in their bones is an unshakable belief that a black man is not a part of their reality, that the chances of my repeating their confidences to anyone who counts in their world is zero.

Other 85 percenters, I have found, are anxious to assure me how liberal they are, that they belong to black organizations such as the N.A.A.C.P. Or that they don't hate blacks at all. Just southern whites, or Jews or Italians or Puerto Ricans. Or that they have nothing but admiration for "good" Negroes.

While waiting to pick up my little red station wagon this evening at the public garage near my office, I was recognized, as often happens, by perhaps a dozen men and women clustered around the cashier. Television fans. All white. One of them was much more candid than the rest. A handsome, well-dressed chap around my age. There was a fuzziness in his voice suggesting that his candor had been poured minutes before from a bottle. If asked to describe his attitude on the race question, I am positive he would say, "A very liberal white liberal."

Well, there in the garage—after joining the enthusiastic chorus of "I watch you every night"—he delivered what he clearly regarded as the compliment supreme:

"If the rest of them were all like you," he said cheerfully, "everything would be all right. No problem at all."

Luckily, I had the presence of mind to short-circuit my automatic response to compliments of almost any sort—as gracious a "thank you" as I can manage. In this case, I clamped my jaws tight, looked away and said nothing. I did not erase my smile, however. A concession I often make in situations like that. Anyone's television career depends on alienating as few viewers as possible. My excuse for not telling that very liberal white liberal what I thought is this: I need the money I am making to maintain that wall of dollars I have built around my family to protect us as much as possible from the whims of Mister Charlie's society.

Had I been facing another "liberal," one who was not one of my fans, I would have told him that the reason "the rest of them" are not like me is that they never get anything like the almost-equal opportunities I have had, that perhaps only a thousand black men in the entire country receive comparable opportunities in a given year, that the other 21,999,000 blacks are virtually locked out of this society, that they are outside looking in. With bitterness, anger and hate.

I wish I could tell you, my son, that the "very liberal white liberal" I met at the garage represents the last breed of tasteless white that is likely to set your teeth on edge. The uncomfortable fact is that the 85 percenters are masters of self-deception; they are also resourceful, coming up periodically with disguises so clever that you are forced to admire their inventiveness. Because of my long experience, however, I am not fooled for a moment by such innocent-sounding gambits as "Some of my best friends are Negroes" or "Frankly, we've never had a Negro guest at our yacht club, but we'd be proud to have you and your wife come out for the weekend."

I also recognize 85 percenters among my closest white associates by their inability to recognize me in an unfamiliar setting. In the office, I am an individual, of course. But elsewhere—even on the street immediately outside the office—I become, in their eyes, just another animated blob of black protoplasm. Which couldn't possibly have any connection with them. It is not that they refuse to see me; their minds simply won't let them if I am not where they expect.

So how do I respond to their snubs, their impersonal confidences, their N.A.A.C.P. cards, their condescension, their insults to nonblack minorities?

I don't.

I let them go their way without challenge; I let them

148

rave on and on without comment. Sometimes they get the point. In any event, I have come to believe that any man who behaves in any of those fashions is a hunky, and well beyond repair. I try to spend as little time as possible in his presence.

Dear Adam,

If you have developed any curiosity at all by now, Adam-Smasher, chances are you are wondering—since Mister Charlie is the meanest man in town 85 percent of the time —why I give any white man the benefit of the doubt.

Well, the lesson began several years ago, before you were born, when the Tall Lady and I were newlyweds. I received a raise in pay from *The New York Times* in 1958. We decided that we could therefore afford a better apartment than our one-and-a-half-room disaster in a slum on the West Side of midtown Manhattan.

Each day we would check the apartments-for-rent ads in *The Times* and divide the likely ones to investigate during our normal routines. But on the third afternoon of our separate searches, the Tall Lady came home in tears.

She had gone to see an apartment that turned out to be an overpriced rattrap. Cracks in the walls, holes in the floor and leaks in the rusted plumbing. This had not been apparent from the ad. It never is.

"I wouldn't live in a place like that," she said between sobs, "if they paid me. But don't you know? When the landlord came upstairs and saw me looking at it, he told me he couldn't rent it to me because the other tenants would complain. Can you believe it? A rattrap like that?"

I believed it. And I never let her go alone after that. I suspect that I would have killed that landlord if I had met him any time soon after seeing my wife in tears. I was as angry with myself as I was with him, I suppose. What kind of man is it who can't protect the woman he loves from humiliating moments like that?

Together we ran into much of the same, with variations, over the next four weeks. Sometimes they told us that the apartment we wanted had been rented a few minutes ago— between the time we had telephoned to be sure it was vacant and the time it took us to get there. At other times we were told that the ad had been cancelled a week before, but was still running by mistake. Or that the price was actually twice as much as advertised. Well beyond our means at the time.

I let them know, as civilly as possible for me, that we knew they were lying. But that didn't solve anything. We grew angrier, more frustrated, with each experience. There seemed a city-wide white conspiracy to keep us from getting out of that slum. Our money, our credit references, our college degrees, our reasonably good manners meant nothing. We finally stopped looking. We could not go through that dehumanizing process indefinitely.

Then came the day that we saw, quite by chance, an ad that said: "Apartments for rent in newly renovated brownstone. Occupancy within one month. Reasonable."

We followed it up, against our better judgment.

The door was open, and the workmen were still in the building, plastering, painting and hammering. They told us that none of the apartments had been rented, and that the landlord would be there within the hour. We picked out the apartment we liked best and waited.

A few minutes later, a well-dressed, middle-aged man showed up. He had to be the landlord. He was white. I got angry the moment I saw him. Another one of those. Before he could begin the expected mealymouthed and well-rehearsed evasion, I practically spat at him:

"We came to rent this apartment you advertised in *The Times*."

The anger in my voice made it sound more like a challenge to a duel.

"But I don't want to waste any time on bullshit. If you don't want to rent to me, I'll be damned if I want to rent from you. Just say so straight out, without beating around the goddamn bush, and we'll leave."

To my astonishment, he didn't get angry. He didn't even get red in the face. In fact, he laughed out loud.

"Hold on a minute," he said cheerfully. "I'm on your side. I can see you've been making the rounds." His smile was open and friendly.

"Yeah, the runarounds," I replied, smiling tentatively.

His name was Jim. The Tall Lady and I lived in his building quite happily ever after for five and a half years. Until we bought the cooperative apartment we live in now. Jim proved to be not only a fair man, but a good friend as well. He and his wife learned to share our enthusiasm for ancient history, science fiction and ballet. We learned to share their appreciation of poetry, Mexican food and modern art. In fact, the Tall Lady began studying painting as a hobby. Among other things, she painted that funny-looking purple tiger and the yellow giraffe that hang in your room over the toy chest.

•

Dear Adam,

You are still too young to recognize it, my son, but this is Christmas time. And yet we have not bought a single new plaything since your birthday.

Neither have we mailed any Christmas cards, nor set up an evergreen tree—fireproof or otherwise. There is no tinsel, no papier-mâché Santa Clauses in our living room. No pink blonde angels—all angels are pink, it seems—suspended by wires from the ceiling. And if we had a fireplace in this apartment, there would be no stockings hung by the chimney with care.

In short, my son, the Tall Lady and I regard Christmas —that is, white society's version of it—as a grand hoax. We refuse to accept their perversion of what should perhaps be a time to reflect on the teachings given to the world long ago by a wise young man called Jesus.

I said young man, not god. It is one thing to recognize wisdom, quite another to build a system of superstition around it. To do that is to lose the wisdom itself. But that is precisely the error Mister Charlie made in this country. If he had not lost the meaning of his god's decrees, he could never have become a slavemaster. In fact, he could never have become Mister Charlie.

Nor could he have turned his god's birthday into a pagan carnival, a time for unloading as much useless junk as possible to as many people as possible at the highest possible price. He calls it the Christmas Spirit.

However, if he sees any conflict between the teachings of his god and his own behavior at Christmas time—or any

153

other time—he manages to ignore it. Just as he kids around with another ritual called Brotherhood Week.

It is our judgment then—the Tall Lady's and mine—that you, my son, should have everything you need and many of the things you simply want, even silly fads, as long as we have the strength to get them. But we will do so at a time of your choosing and ours. Not when Mister Charlie is having a Christmas sale. Which usually means that he has jacked up his prices 50 to 150 percent.

The only elements of Christmas that we accept are those principles of human conduct that Mister Charlie's god left behind. We observe them as best we can. Not only at Christmas time. And not to bribe our way into that never-never land Mister Charlie calls heaven when we die. But because those principles are sensible and humane.

Dear Adam,

This is a night of reflection for your parents—the ending of the old year; the beginning of the new. It has become a tradition with us to mark the occasion alone together at home, reflecting on where our lives have been and where we would like them to go. There is always champagne, of course. Everything worthy of a toast, in the past, the present and the future, is given its due. Including my birthday, which arrives the day after New Year's.

At one point in our rambling review with clinking wine glasses this evening, the Tall Lady gave me a lower grade as a husband and a father for 1967 than I had received for the year 1966.

"It's not that you've changed for the worse or anything," she explained. "It's just that you weren't around as much. You worked either six days or seven days a week all year long, and spent a lot of your days off speaking to strangers. I know you think you owe something to those kids out there—that they need you. But so does Adam. And so do I."

I nodded, then pointed out that the sixth day of my work week meant extra money.

"We'd rather have extra you," she replied.

Resolved: Effective at once, I will drop my sixth day, as anyone in my office is allowed to do. And limit my speaking engagements to one a month.

We bumped our glasses again and drank to that.

Later, I gave the Tall Lady a higher grade as a wife

and Adam-watcher than she had ever received in all our years together. She had devoted only two months of the old year to rehearsing and performing with a dance company on Broadway. Which meant that she had given more of herself to you and me than we should reasonably demand. There is a Tall Lady that exists apart from us just as there is a you that exists apart from your parents.

"Why don't we use baby-sitters more often this year?" I suggested. "Get you out of the house more and perhaps back to dancing. Certainly two or three classes a week for openers."

"Oh, I'd love that," she said with excitement. "That's the best idea you've had so far in 1968."

She raised her glass, then stopped it short, frowning. "I just remembered," she said. "With you taking a cut in pay, maybe we shouldn't add to our expenses. Between the classes and the baby-sitters and the extra meals we'll be eating away from home . . ."

"Baby, we can't take it with us," I said. "So let's spend it for a heavenly time in this life—maybe the only one there is."

We drank to that, too.

Our next toast, several minutes later, was to you, my son. For the happiness you had brought to our lives. We congratulated ourselves for having waited more than ten years before becoming parents. We had indulged our wildest selfish whims in all of that time—traveling and generally living it up. We had had the time and the money. We knew how to spend them both. Which meant we hadn't brought you into our carnival until we were ready and eager for the changes you would bring. Diapers and all.

156

The Tall Lady put it like this: "Adam hasn't taken anything away from our lives that we weren't ready to give up. Instead, he adds something special—to me as a person, to you and also to . . . what we've always had between us."

"Skoal!"

Dear Adam,

In a previous letter, my son—describing Mister Charlie's futile search for "safe" Negro leaders—I deliberately did not mention the black madman who first helped the Tall Lady and me to realize that our brains had been dipped in shame and washed with wrong advice, that we had been trying to stand apart from black folk in an effort to appease Mister Charlie. That black leader, our personal hero, was by no means "safe." I refer, of course, to the man the late Malcolm X had become shortly before he was killed a few years ago. He was a cut above most men we have met, and we want him to stand alone in your mind.

The man Malcolm X had become was the one black man I could not argue with, even now. Although I knew him as a news source—someone to be interviewed from time to time—I did not fully recognize his greatness or his wisdom until long after his death.

But now it's clear. Malcolm X was truly the maddest of us all. Also, the most dangerous man Mister Charlie has had to face in this century.

Malcolm X evolved. First he was Malcolm Little, an outlaw, a dope addict and a convict. Then he became Minister Malcolm, a high-ranking member of the Black Muslims, preaching complete separation from whites. And, finally, he became Malcolm X, the tallest black man alive —an independent messiah.

He dropped his blanket definition of whites as "blue-eyed devils." Instead, he defined Mister Charlie as "the

Ku Klux Klan, the White Citizens Councils and other white people who practice discrimination and segregation against black people." That covered most whites, of course.

He stopped urging black folk to hate whites simply because they were white; but to hate them rather because of what they were doing. "I'm going to create an awareness among black people," he once explained, "of what has been done to them. This awareness will produce an abundance of energy, both positive and negative."

That scared the pants off Mister Charlie. An even bigger scare was yet to come.

Malcolm X began traveling abroad, picking up new ideas and potential allies among Africans, Arabs and Chinese. Mister Charlie could see a black-brown-yellow peril on the horizon. Malcolm X was linking the American racial problem with what he called "a global rebellion of the oppressed against the oppressors, the exploited against the exploiters."

His words were followed by political action at the United Nations. It shook Mister Charlie to the core. Black African states, condemning U.S. intervention in the Congo, compared the U.S. role in the Congo—helping the side of imperialism—to the treatment of black people in Mississippi.

"The African nations," Malcolm X said afterward, "are represented by intelligent statesmen. It was only a matter of time before they would see that they would have to intervene in behalf of twenty-two million black Americans who are their brothers and sisters."

Mister Charlie has always been afraid of the 700,000,-000 Chinese who have long memories of his one-sided dealings with Orientals. He found new cause for fear when

Malcolm X began rubbing elbows with diplomats from Peking.

"What do I think of Red China in relation to Afro-Americans?" he said. "Well, I think it's good to have centers of power on our side that are not controlled by either Washington, London or Paris. . . . Because the only time Mister Charlie gives black people a break is when he has something on the outside of his house that he's worried about. Then he lets those on the inside of his house have a little more leeway than normal."

And if that wasn't enough to unnerve the white power structure, this was: By simple arithmetic Malcolm X added the nonwhite populations in Africa, Asia and Latin America and came up with a nonwhite majority. "When the people in these different areas see that their problem and our problem is the same problem," he declared, "the oppressed people of this earth will approach our problem not as a minority, but as a majority—a majority that can *demand*, not beg."

Malcolm X was pointing to what seems an inevitable future. Which causes the racist mind to boggle. He devoted his last days to teaching black folk to defend themselves, not turn the other cheek. Also, he was forging a nonwhite alliance around the world. The first victory in his dream would be political. He dreamed of the day when the nonwhite coalition would be strong enough to put the United States on trial before the United Nations—before the world—for its crimes against humanity.

Could there be any doubt of guilt?

Now Malcolm X is dead. I don't know what will become of his dream. Many black folk who still mourn his death—including the Tall Lady—are convinced that though black fingers pulled the triggers in the assassination of Malcolm X, Mister Charlie was involved in the plot.

I doubt it. All wise men have enemies among fools, I have learned.

But I have absolutely no doubt that when Mister Charlie heard Malcolm X was dead, he smiled.

Dear Adam,

Now that I have cut my broadcasting week from six nights a week to five—as I promised the Tall Lady—I'm finding time to *watch* television for a change. Tonight I saw something that increased my respect for it. Although neutral on the racial question, the TV screen is an effective propaganda agent in the cause of the Black Revolution.

What I saw was a film report of an art auction uptown. Oil paintings by some of the most celebrated artists of the century were being sold to the highest bidders. Picassos, Mirós, Klees and Chagalls. More than a hundred private collectors were taking part. All wore tuxedos or shimmering evening gowns. None raised an eyebrow or checked his bankbook when the auctioneer started the bidding on some paintings at fifty thousand dollars. They simply made notes on their catalogues, then signaled their bids with undramatic gestures. It seemed like a boring party game.

The final price for several of the forty-seven paintings they bought was well above two hundred thousand dollars.

Everyone in the game was white. Black folk were not barred from the auction. At least, not directly. But this not uncommon event casually dramatized how black folk are automatically shut out. They don't qualify for admission because they are denied a chance to earn the price of it.

Television—just another toy to you right now, my son—gives testimony like that around the clock. It is helping—quite accidentally—to set a slightly better stage for your tomorrow. Without even preaching about right and wrong, television can't avoid making a big point for our side now and then. It reveals a reality hard to deny. It makes it more difficult for many white folk to remain comfortable with fuzzy notions about what is going on, say, in New York City or Mississippi.

It shows the smooth green lawns and handsome one-family houses in the all-white suburbs; the run-down overcrowded tenements in the black concentration camps.

It shows the nearly all-white conventions of top business executives and professional men; the nearly all-black conventions of pullman car porters.

It also shows white men and women—wearing tailored fashions, diamonds and furs—having fun attending the theater, the opera or a charity ball; black men and women —wearing servants' uniforms—opening doors for whites, cooking for whites, mixing drinks for whites, cleaning up the messes made by whites and accepting tips from whites.

In short, television quite accidentally dramatizes the reality of two American societies—separate and unequal.

And so it is that month by month as the Black Revolution advances inch by inch, some members of white society come to recognize the depth of their crime against the Negro.

That is why in 1967—more than a hundred years after Lincoln's Emancipation Proclamation—President Lyndon B. Johnson could say publicly: "Freedom is not a prize reserved for white Americans in their private enclaves of affluence." He had seen the TV screen's proof that most white Americans behave as if freedom had nothing to do with nonwhites. There is sufficient evidence in the fact that most television programs deal with happy whites with happy problems happily solved within thirty minutes by a beautiful and clever white female; or a handsome white avenger on horseback. So no one had to tell the President that something was drastically amiss. That fact was also obvious to the people he was talking about.

In that same year, you will have learned by now, my son, the President appointed a Commission on Civil Disorders to find why black men were burning down a substantial part of this country. Actually, everyone knew the answer, deep down. But it was never mentioned in public, and therefore did not seem terrible enough or real enough to be disturbing. No one was really surprised when the President's Commission reported in 1968: "The main cause of the riots was white racism. . . . What white Americans can't seem to understand, but what Negroes can never forget, is that white people are deeply involved in the ghetto. It is created by whites; maintained by white institutions, and condoned by white society."

No one was surprised, because television had already made it clear. It showed how whites lived in this country and how blacks simply existed.

Television had also prepared white minds by providing a coast-to-coast forum for the few men in my time in this country—black and white—who had been able to purge their brains of civilization's garbage and debris. Through TV, they were able to help other brains take the cure.

An angry black man named Cecil Brown—with whom I grew up in Milwaukee—recently said to the whole nation: "As long as only Negro rights are being denied, you don't hear the whites saying anything at all about lawlessness. But when Negroes become so frustrated and fed up that they destroy a little private property, then the whites cry loud and clear that 'we've got to put a stop to this lawlessness.'"

164

Scores of TV entertainments, like many you've probably seen around national holidays, praised the white dissenters who wrenched this country from the British. These also helped prepare white folk for the truth about themselves. They were told by H. Rap Brown, the black revolutionary: "Why was it heroic for a white man named Patrick Henry to say 'Give me liberty or give me death' and un-American for a black man to say it? I say this country was built on violence. I say violence is as American as cherry pie."

Other television programs showing the misery of "poor white trash" in the hills of Appalachia perhaps led well-heeled whites to wonder why black folk don't bear their miseries with the same dignity and patience. Eventually, television also explained that the difference between being a poor white and being a poor black is that the whites have no reason to feel that the system conspires to keep them poor. A black revolutionary named Bayard Rustin put it this way on television:

"I do not believe there are riots because there are bad schools; not because there are slums; nor because there is unemployment. These are hardships, and men are capable of enduring hardships. But what they cannot endure is hardships where hope is absent. And in this society, a black man does not have hope that tomorrow or next week or even next year he will have a chance to get a good education, a good job and decent housing."

Still other TV programs—especially the panel shows involving members of the white power structure—show that whites are fond of making promises. But television also shows that the promises are not kept; that nothing significant follows to change the conditions that drive black

165

men to violence. The evidence of this had been displayed on television screens hundreds of times by mid-1967, when a white Roman Catholic priest, the Rev. James Groppi, told the nation quite matter-of-factly:

"If you want the black man to give up violence in his fight for freedom and dignity, you must prove to him that the white power structure will respond to nonviolent methods. But it seems to me it's already too late to prove it. The Rap Browns and Stokely Carmichaels have already given up on protest marches and freedom songs."

All of these bits of truth, reinforced by television, whether it tries to or not, contribute to each new inch of freedom the black man gains. Another state legislature passes a bill outlawing racial discrimination in housing. And, finally, the Federal Government does the same on a national scale.

However, this progress is not so great as it may seem. The law passed to wipe out a long-standing injustice is rarely enforced with the zeal that would be seen if the victims were, say, Lithuanians, rather than Negroes. And even when some especially raw injustice—such as the murder of a civil rights worker in the South—causes a public outrage that demands prosecution of the Ku Klux Klansmen responsible, it is a rare day when the courts, usually with white judges and juries, let the guilty men feel the full weight of the law.

Perhaps the classic example of this double standard is the 1954 Supreme Court decision outlawing school segregation across the land. Today, fourteen years after the Supreme Court told white schools to desegregate with "all deliberate speed," the school segregation picture is unimproved. Just last year, Ramsey Clark, the United States

Attorney General, said: "As a direct result of housing segregation, there is more school segregation than ever before in our history."

Why, I can hear you ask, have such promises been kept in full rarely, if indeed they are kept at all?

My guess is that there is a kind of accidental balance among whites; for every one who is somehow persuaded to scale down his commitment to white supremacy, the built-in patterns of white supremacy in this society somehow persuade hundreds of others that their systematic mistreatment of blacks is not a question of justice or injustice, not a question of right or wrong. It is merely the natural order.

Dear Adam-Smasher,

Your adopted Uncle Julian joined us this afternoon on that silly playground across the street as he often does. He echoed some of the guesses I've made about your tomorrow. If you survive that silly playground, that is.

"I saw your newscast last night," he said. "Got quite a kick out of that story out of Cleveland. My man Stokes is turning out to be a one-man fortress of black power."

Uncle Julian—"The Uncle" as you sometimes call him —was talking about Mayor Carl Stokes, a Negro. As Mayor of Cleveland, Stokes theoretically controls the large black vote in that city. And the film on my news program had shown white politicians wooing this black man for support in campaigns for the Presidential nomination.

Julian and I stood together about five feet behind you as you climbed among those odd-looking steel constructions, concrete shapes and plastic enclosures on the playground. It is like nothing we had seen as youngsters. We stood behind you, as we usually do, trying to give the impression that we are not hovering. But both of us were half-poised on the balls of our feet, ready to spring forward.

"It wouldn't surprise me," Uncle Julian went on, "if Stokes wound up as somebody's running mate on a Presidential ticket in 1976."

I nodded, then caught my breath. Your feet had slipped off one of those tricky steel shapes. But you held on with your hands, and regained full control.

I breathed again.

"Why the hell do they put things like that in playgrounds anyway?" I asked for the umpteenth time. "What ever happened to swings, slides, monkey ladders and sandboxes? Things a father can understand."

My best friend laughed. "Ah, this is a brave new world your son is growing up in," he said. "And what you see is progress. These things may look strange to us, but they don't frighten Adam in the least. He has no idea of what playgrounds were like when you and I were his age."

I knew he was right. But I still didn't like it.

"Getting back to Stokes," I said. "I think you're right about a black Vice President. The same thought has occurred to me. But your timetable is off. It won't be Stokes, and it won't happen in 1976. But it will happen in the twenty-first century by the time Adam is as old as we are now. Who knows? It could be Adam himself."

"Congratulations," Uncle Julian said, laughing. He placed an imaginary television mike under my chin. "And would you tell our viewers, sir, how it feels to be the father of a future Vice President?"

We laughed together, impressed with our own boldness. Yet, daring as we were, my son, your children may one day be bold enough to believe that a black man could become President.

Your Uncle Julian was perhaps more flabbergasted than I. He and his older brother had grown up in Norfolk, Virginia—part of the "land behind the sun." He is fond of telling of the time when Mister Charlie burned a cross—the symbol of the Ku Klux Klan—on their front yard one night. His family had just bought a house in a white neighborhood in Norfolk.

"The next day," he recalls, "when my daddy came home

from work, he brought three new rifles into the house. With plenty of ammunition. He took my brother and me out into the backyard and taught us how to shoot. Man, we shot up some tin cans that day—in broad daylight so everybody would know what we were doing.

"But from that day on, nobody burned anything on our front yard. Nobody bothered us at all."

Dear Adam,

My prediction of wider horizons for black folk in your time perhaps sounded more optimistic than I intended. Not that my prediction went too far. But it should have been tempered with an important qualification:

Black participation in all areas of this society—jobs, housing, education and politics—will increase much faster than the acceptance of change by either race. Even when the day of full participation becomes possible—when all the roadblocks have been removed—black folk will need time to adjust. They will have to overcome their basic distrust and hostility toward whites, to learn to believe that the new America is not a big lie like the old one. Right now, those suspicions are born in our bones. Black men of the twenty-first century will need two or three generations to learn to believe that the newly opened doors are not a refinement of Mister Charlie's favorite prank: declaring a door open and then slamming it in any black face that does not belong to a superman.

Only when that legacy of distrust has been forgotten by a distant *second* generation of blacks to enjoy full participation all their lives, will black folk truly be free. Only then will they begin behaving like the models of middle-class decency that Mister Charlie demands they be now while treating most blacks like animals.

Some distant generation of Mister Charlie's descendants will also have to overcome old habits that seem rooted in white souls: Responding to myths about black folk instead of responding to the individual black person they happen to be facing.

All of this is to say, my son, that even if you were to become Vice President in the twenty-first century, you would probably still have to cope with a ridiculous amount of frustration and rejection that had nothing to do with you as a man.

Only last night, your daddy received another reminder that regardless of what laws are passed in Washington, D.C., to expand my acceptance in this society—and regardless of my credentials as a black man who has matched Mister Charlie in every game—real democracy depends on what happens day by day between individual members of different races.

I had just left the studio after my late newscast. I needed a taxi to get home to our apartment in Lower Manhattan.

At the corner of Broadway and 49th Street, I hailed an empty Yellow Cab as it approached from 50th Street, going downtown. The white man at the wheel seemed not to hear or see me. He passed me by.

I told myself, as I often do in these situations, that I should not jump to the conclusion that I was bypassed because I am black. After all, everyone in New York City gets passed up by a taxicab from time to time. It was possible that the man hadn't seen me.

Within two minutes, however, as three more empty Yellow Cabs turned me down, I was swearing under my breath. The bastards won't let you live! Each of those three white drivers had seen me. I knew it. As they approached from 50th Street, each swerved his cab briefly in my direction at the curb; then, upon seeing that I was black, each turned his wheels the other way, looked straight ahead, pretended to be deaf and tromped down hard on the accelerator.

But the fourth cab in that hate parade had to stop about twenty yards past me, just across the 49th Street intersection, because of a red light. The traffic on Broadway was backed up from the light at 48th Street, a block ahead. I walked across the intersection and reached for the door handle on the cab. The driver turned and tried to push down the button that would lock it. But I was faster on the draw. As I climbed into the back seat, he shouted a barrage of insults and curses.

"And besides," he ended, "I'm going off duty right now!"

I refused to budge. "Then why in the hell didn't you flash your goddamn off-duty sign?" I yelled. Then I slammed the door behind me. "If you don't take me where I want to go," I threatened, reading his name and number on the license affixed to the dashboard, "I'll turn your ass in at the Hack Bureau. You know goddamn well what you did is against the law."

The driver—let's call him Fred—was stopped in midsentence by the sound of my voice. Not by what I said.

"Oh, it's *you*," he said sheepishly. "I didn't recognize you at first until I heard your voice. I'd know that voice anywhere. On the moon even. You really do a great job with the news. I watch you every night when I'm not out hacking so late like tonight and . . ."

I said nothing. Fred kept chattering. I was more than a little uncertain about how to take it.

The light turned green at 48th Street. Traffic on Broadway began moving, and Fred moved with it. Still talking, still mixing flatteries with apologies.

"Gee, I'd give anything if I hadn't made that mistake," he went on. "I'm really and truly sorry. And you know what makes it so funny is that I've had you in my cab

173

before. I picked you up just outside the studio one night maybe five, six months ago. You're going to the edge of Chinatown, right? I took you there that time. And like I told you then, me and my wife we watch you all the time. Man, wait'll I tell her I had you in my cab again. She's always saying how what a handsome guy you are on TV. Sexy and all that, she says. And she gave me a bad time for not getting your autograph the last time I took you home. This ride is on me, by the way. I couldn't think of taking any money after what happened. It's a real pleasure and thrill just having you in my cab. And . . ."

I didn't feel flattered. I felt angry, indignant and embarrassed. Gradually, however, Fred's nonstop apology did confuse the situation. Should I be a nice guy and accept his apology? Should I spit in his face? Should I chew him out? Should I give him a calm little lecture on how being treated like that was the stuff that drove black men to madness—the stuff that riots are made of? Or should I say nothing at all and simply take my case to the Hack Bureau?

Finally, perhaps two miles from where we had met, Fred paused to breathe and light a smoke. He passed the pack over his shoulder. I took one and lit up, too.

"Gee, I really wish that hadn't happened back there," he said again.

"It's all right, Fred," I said. "Let's forget it. But remember it the next time you see a black man standing on a corner. And try to imagine how you'd feel if something like that happened to you almost every other time you left your house."

Fred apologized again. And again. And again.

"It's all right," I said. "Let's forget it."

174

When we got to the corner near my apartment, the meter read $1.85. Fred wouldn't accept my money.

"Oh, no," he said. "This is on me. A real pleasure having you in my cab."

I hesitated, still uncertain. He sounded as if he were truly repentant. But was he really? And if so, did it matter? Could he have been thinking that he had tried to pass up a black man who was too well known to be called a liar if the case ever went before the Hack Bureau?

"I can't take your money," Fred went on. "But I would appreciate an autograph for my missus, if you don't mind."

Here it was. The right moment and exactly the right place to spit in his face. But I couldn't do it. Let your triumph, I told myself, be the knowledge that no matter what they do, they can't turn you into something just as ugly.

I signed the pad he offered. "Here you are," I said as evenly as possible for me. "And good night."

Fred thanked me and made one final apology before driving off.

As I started walking toward the entrance of our apartment building, I had a curious sense of having lost something of myself. And I knew that I would never get it back.

Dear Adam,

We have just lived through the longest night of our lives. The black patron saint, the Rev. Dr. Martin Luther King, Jr., was assassinated, mourned and buried. We also survived the violent aftermath of black brothers by the thousands blindly searching for revenge.

Dr. King's passage from living symbol to entombed martyr required only six unaccountably sunny days. The passage of black vigilantes from stunned mourners to bitter marauders and finally back to men required a week of accountably ugly nights. The dark skies over a hundred-odd cities across this nation glowed red with the fires of black passion.

Now, after the fact, my brain cannot sort out the separate events. The calendar fixed in my mind simply stopped turning its pages.

My main impression is that we watched the complete horror from beginning to end, sitting slumped in front of our television screen. Your adopted Uncle Julian and Aunt Mary were with us all the time. Or so it seems. I realize that we must have eaten meals, changed your diapers and gone our separate ways now and then.

One of my first clear thoughts, when shock had ebbed to dull acceptance, was quite selfish. I was glad that I would not have to go on the air that black Thursday night to broadcast details of his death. Friday would also be a day off. Which would give me time to regain my pose as a newscaster. Uninvolved, cool and unafraid of tomorrow.

"Look at that," your Uncle Julian said in a hushed whisper that first evening in our apartment. Or was it the second or the fifth? "That must be where it happened."

His voice seemed to come from a cavern a great distance away. And so the long night began to unfold like an erratic newsreel of another time, another place and other people long ago.

All of us disengage from our private thoughts. We refocus on the screen. There we see an ordinary motel in Memphis. It does not seem a fitting place for such a man to die. There also is the dingy rooming house across the street where the white assassin pulled the trigger. We don't see the killing on the screen. But the details of that moment are so vividly described over and over that we soon come to believe that we were there.

In seeing him fall, on the screen of my imagination, I am haunted by a familiar recollection. He is two weeks younger than I. For years, as I had observed his courage and sacrifices, I felt ashamed. Nothing in the total of my existence can begin to approach even a single day of his life. I can never become too proud of myself, knowing that.

The screen flickers. The picture changes in rapid succession. A series of familiar faces—black and white, drawn and strained—pay homage to a champion of humanity. President Lyndon B. Johnson, a reformed Texan, is among them. Almost as one voice, measured and sober, they praise Dr. King as perhaps the greatest man of his century.

It's strange. Now that the man is dead, there seems to be a conspiracy of pretense among whites. They imply that they and almost everybody else had been on his side all along. Little attention is given to certain facts. Like President Johnson's quietly urging Martin Luther King,

177

through third parties, to drop his plans for a massive march of poor people on Washington, D.C., to demand a fair share of the richest nation in history. And what about former President Harry S Truman, describing Dr. King as "a troublemaker"? What about J. Edgar Hoover, director of the F.B.I., publicly branding Dr. King as "the most notorious liar in the country"?

There is also a pretense that a single sick mind has killed this good black man. Then some wise old heads with black faces, long memories and angry voices appear on my television screen. Together, almost as if they have rehearsed, they smash the white pretense. A black Baptist minister says in his pulpit: "It was not a single twisted mind that killed Dr. Martin Luther King, Jr. The man who pulled the trigger knew full well that he was doing the bidding of white society."

The four of us sitting there in the semidarkness of the living room are not religious in the Baptist's sense. We are therefore greatly surprised to hear ourselves say in concert, "Amen."

Moments later—or was it earlier?—we see a series of forgotten film clips showing Martin Luther King trying to walk peacefully through the suburban badlands. Forbidden territory like Cicero, Illinois. We see again the pretty faces of white housewives, twisted with hate, as they curse and spit upon him. The police make no move to stop them. Although we then recall what's going to happen next, we still suck in our breaths when we see it. He stumbles and falls, blood trickling from a head wound. A rock has found its mark.

We have not yet recovered from that blow when we see

him attacked by snarling dogs. They seem huge and invincible on short leashes held by white policemen. He seems small by comparison. And close to death.

The screen flickers again. We are relieved, irrationally, to see that he has survived. But now he is in handcuffs. Being led off to jail by white policemen. We hear an alien voice from another planet. It tells us that Dr. King was jailed thirty times. For leading peaceful protests against injustice.

The four of us in the living room sob openly. There is no attempt to comfort one another. There is no attempt to hide our tears.

For us—and for millions of others across this nation—the long ordeal is just beginning. We find ourselves being tortured anew by the sound of the dead man's voice. We see and hear him speak memorable words of compassion. Which will live as long as men anywhere in any time believe in truth and freedom.

There he is speaking at a church in Memphis on the night before his death. His eyes, his words, his tone of voice seem to tell us he knows he's near the end. He has lived with threats of violent death for thirteen years, he reminds us. And new threats have reached his ears in Memphis.

"Well, I don't know what will happen now. We've got some difficult days ahead. But it really doesn't matter with me now. Because I've been to the mountain top. . . . And I've looked over, and I've seen the promised land.

"I may not get there with you," he says with love and passion, "but I want you to know tonight that we as a people will get to the promised land!"

The screen flickers again. Now we see him in another southern pulpit months ago. He tells us his idea of a fitting eulogy—the words he hopes are said at his funeral.

"Don't say I won the Nobel Peace Prize," he shouts with evangelistic fury. "Don't mention my other awards. Just say I tried to help somebody!"

But the speech that hits us hardest, almost physically, is the one he made—and makes again, on our screen—in the summer of 1963. We all of us are transported back to that sweltering day in August when he led us and 210,000 others—black and white—on a march in Washington, D.C. To appeal to the conscience of a nation. We strain our eyes at the flickering screen, trying to get a glimpse of ourselves in the tremendous multitude that stretches before the Lincoln Memorial in Washington.

"I have a dream," the dead man thunders with fervor. "That one day in the red hills of Georgia the sons of former slaves and the sons of former slavemasters will sit down together at the table of common brotherhood! I have a dream . . ."

We feel something wrench in our hearts. We feel a sense of loss for black men everywhere. For all men. For all time to come. Yet all we can do is weep again.

The screen flickers. Now we see and hear some of the great thinkers of our time. They agree that his dream and his nonviolent methods were right in the cause of justice. They also express the hope that his death will shock all whites into reason and simple common sense. To end the nightmare of white racism he fought.

None of us in our living room is naive enough to hear their hopes as prophecy. Our memories are too vivid. Gratefully, we give our eyes and ears to a series of wise old heads—black and white—whose memories are equal to our own. They remind us of white society's impressive show of remorse after previous black tragedies in the 1960's.

We relive the assassination of a black rights champion named Medgar Evers in Jackson, Mississippi, in 1963.

We are reminded that Jimmy Lee Jackson, a black protest marcher, was gunned down in Marion, Mississippi.

We weep again for four small black girls killed in Albany, Georgia, in the bombing of a Negro church.

Our tears are not only for the victims but for ourselves. Also, for other black victims we know deep down are yet to be killed in much the same way for exactly the same reason.

Our hopes for tomorrow sink lower than ever. Then the screen flickers again. Martin Luther King accepts the Nobel Peace Prize in Stockholm, Sweden, and tells us to keep faith with him:

"I refuse to accept the idea that man is mere flotsam and jetsam in the river of life which surrounds him. I refuse to accept the view that mankind is so tragically bound to the starless midnight of racism and war that the bright daybreak of peace and brotherhood can never become a reality . . . I believe that unarmed truth and unconditional love will have the final word in reality."

We are awed again. Wondering how this giant of a man managed to hang on to so much more of his humanity than perhaps any man still alive.

Yet none of us in the living room pretends to forget our basic disagreement with the dead man. Without exception, in brief comments, we reaffirm a common stand: There is something indecent about asking black men—facing ferocious apostles of racism—forever to turn the other cheek.

We are therefore gratified as the screen dissolves to scenes of black folk giving Mister Charlie a grand opportunity for turning the other cheek for a change. His stores that gouge and cheat us in the ghettos are smashed, looted, burned. The ancient ruins he rents to us—and refuses to repair—are gutted by hungry flames.

Seeing this, we feel no guilt or shame. On the contrary. We feel a sense of pride. These are nothing more than counterattacks—and the closest thing we have seen to real justice in our lifetimes. Besides, this is the stuff that impresses Mister Charlie. As turning the other cheek never does. Tomorrow, he may move—perhaps a fraction of an inch—out of fear.

The screen flickers. And there, standing in the middle of a burned-out ghetto in Cincinnati, a scowling black man tells a white reporter like it is:

"If white people wants this burnin' and lootin' to stop, they got to start treatin' black people like human bein's. Cause that's what they are—human bein's."

Again our living room resounds with a chorus, "Amen!"

We understand that the violence is only distantly related to the murder of Martin Luther King. The burning and looting in his name is profane, irrational, insane. But this, we remind one another, is the response of people who have been brutalized by a hostile and brutal majority all their lives. If you treat a man as if he is something less than a human being, eventually he becomes something less. Something ugly.

If black violence is a reaction to brutal treatment, the question then is: Who or what has brutalized Mister Charlie? The answer is obvious to all of us: In doing what he

182

does to black folks, he has perpetuated something less than human, something ugly in himself.

Again the screen flickers. More processions, eulogies and hymns to the martyr. In them we see a clue to the one truly significant boon from his sacrifice. He has given us Black Thursday. It is to be a moment in time every year for withdrawing from Mister Charlie's world. To reaffirm our identity as a black people. Also, to remember how far we have come with his guidance, and to recharge our spirits for the long run we still have to make on our own. Black Thursday will become to us what Saint Patrick's Day is to the Irish. What Columbus Day is to Italians. What Rosh ha-Shana means to the Jews.

The four of us vow to set ourselves apart from white society on Black Thursday every April. We are hopeful that black folks everywhere will do the same.

Suddenly, the screen jerks us back, for the exquisite finale of our ordeal. We wince. There sits the dead man's widow. She seems lovelier than ever in her grief. But from the tense way she holds herself erect we can sense that she is clinging to poise by her fingernails.

The screen flickers. Another lovely mourner, Mrs. John F. Kennedy, comes into view. Another civilized woman widowed too early by the poison in the collective mind of this society. We wonder aloud whether these tragic figures must remain forever wed to disembodied legends.

Eventually, we are swept by the screen into the mournful trek to the cemetery. His coffin lies on the bed of a creaking mule-drawn cart. A symbol of his commitment to the poor. This, too, is more than we can bear.

At last they lower his body—and a part of us—into the

grave. We will weep yet again upon reading the epitaph engraved on his white marble tomb:

> *"Free at last, free at last*
> *Thank God Almighty*
> *I'm free at last."*

Dear Adam,

On at least one occasion in his lifetime that I know of, the great man I mourned in the preceding letter—Dr. Martin Luther King, Jr.—displayed in private a mild streak of black chauvinism. It was not apparent in his public image. I tell you this story because your daddy brought out that streak.

The occasion was a news conference I covered a few years ago as a television street reporter, on the grounds of Gracie Mansion. That's the official residence of New York City's Mayor. Dr. King had just finished a closed meeting that afternoon with Mayor Robert F. Wagner, Jr., inside the mansion, discussing ways and means of preventing a racial explosion in the city that summer.

All news media had been barred. Now a small army of us were waiting outside in the driveway to catch Dr. King —our cameras, microphones, lights, tape recorders, pens and pads at the ready. There were seven television crews— four men in each—including mine. Plus a dozen radio reporters, their engineers and at least a dozen legmen from the wire services and the daily press. No one said so, but all of us knew that this interview was going to be what we call in the trade "a gang bang"—a raucous, undignified scramble of questions, with every man for himself. We stood there in a tight knot, joking with friends among our competitors, but ready to pounce.

Finally, Dr. King emerged from Gracie Mansion, some fifty yards away. He was flanked by a staff aide, the Rev.

Wyatt Walker. Then suddenly—from nowhere, it seemed
—one of the cleverest television reporters in town, John
Tillman of WPIX, also appeared at Dr. King's side. His
crew was waiting in the crowd, close to my elbow in fact.
And John was leading the great man to the rest of us. It
was a popular trick in our profession; and Tillman—who
had pioneered TV reporting as the first street man in New
York City in the late 1940's—had thought of it first this
day. By sneaking around the mansion and meeting Dr.
King at the foot of the steps, he guaranteed himself an advantage, a place next to Dr. King when the questioning
began.

The rest of us, feeling grudging admiration to a man,
began moving up the driveway to intercept, dragging our
microphones and cables. And jockeying for position along
the way.

Dr. King's aide, Wyatt Walker, stepped aside, knowing
who the main attraction was. A hand from the crowd
reached over my shoulder, passing a WPIX microphone to
Tillman, who was pressing close on Dr. King's right. Immediately, I elbowed a couple of rival reporters off balance
and planted myself at Dr. King's left. Now Tillman and
I were in the best possible positions for the interview.

There was a roar of curses and grumbles from the ranks
behind us. Because the object of the game in street reporting is to get your face and your microphone into the picture
with the man being interviewed. To guarantee that he will
have to respond to at least a couple of your questions. Some
TV stations refused to pay the standard interview fee for
assignments where reporters failed to get their faces or their
voices on the film.

It was natural also—since I was the only black man in

186

that jungle that day—that all of the bitching from the rear should be aimed at me. My name was shouted at least twenty times with demands that I move out of somebody's line of vision.

"You're blocking our camera," one would charge.

"You're not made of glass, you know," someone else would declare.

And still another would shout, "We're not going to let you get away with this, no matter what."

I refused to budge. "What the hell," I shouted back. "Just do the best you can. I'm just doing my job." I also tried to shift some of their indignation to John Tillman. But no one paid any attention. It was me they wanted to move. It was an impasse, and the start of the interview was delayed at least five minutes.

Dr. King waited patiently. He said nothing. His eyes looked straight ahead, not focused on anything in particular. His dark features were, as usual, placid, composed and detached. At times the pushing from the rear shoved me hard against his shoulder. But I shoved back at my colleagues and maintained my position by sheer strength. I couldn't have held it, however, without adroit assistance from the three white allies in my crew—the cameraman, the soundman and the lightman—close behind.

When it finally became obvious that I would not move an inch without a fight—which there probably would have been if our target had been anyone but the black apostle of nonviolence—they stopped shouting. That old pro—John Tillman—filled the first second of silence with a general order to the rest of us. "Start the cameras." And in his very next breath, before the rest of us bird dogs could react, he posed the first question to Dr. King. It was a long, paragraph-type question, of course, with the point of it in the last two sentences. Tillman was a real pro. His complicated question gave the cameras the necessary seven seconds to get up to recording speed.

I managed to blurt the next two questions and received what I regarded as the kernel of the story Dr. King had to tell that day. Tillman jumped back in with the next question. After that, we graciously allowed the other reporters in the rear to stick in a question now and then. But, basically, it was our news conference—Tillman's and mine—almost as much as Dr. King's.

After perhaps twenty questions, the great man begged to be excused. He barely had time to reach the airport to catch a flight to Washington. He stepped into a waiting limousine with Wyatt Walker.

As the car pulled out of the driveway, the camera crews began to break down their gear and pack up. Once again, I was the target of angry threats and epithets. I answered none and offered no excuses. There was no need to. I had gotten what I came for—on film—and a motorcycle courier was now standing by to rush it to the lab. The grumbling from my colleagues didn't bother me in the least. It was a normal part of the business. Sooner or later, everybody in television news goes through a thing like that.

It was perhaps two weeks later that I saw the Rev. Wyatt Walker again—Dr. King was not present—at a news conference in Harlem. Just before it began, he called me aside to say this:

"I thought you'd like to know that Dr. King got a big kick out of that riot you almost started at Gracie Mansion."

"Oh, really?" I said with a laugh. "What did he say?"

"Well, as we were driving off, he said, 'Did you see the way that black reporter stood his ground? The next time you see that fella you tell him for me that I was mighty proud.'"

Dear Adam,

Just as your daddy and most black mourners foresaw a week ago—the day of Dr. King's funeral—Mister Charlie was back at the same old stand today. Business as usual.

My newscast tonight included two items worth keeping in mind whenever you happen to see Mister Charlie shedding crocodile tears.

The New York City Commission on Human Rights lost its legal fight to examine the membership records of the New York Athletic Club. The idea was to verify the obvious truth that the club bars black men. But the Manhattan Supreme Court accepted the club's argument that its rights as a private organization were more important to the concept of a democratic society than the rights of a minority race. Of course, the court said it in a roundabout way. But then, Mister Charlie always kids around with words at such times.

Keep in mind also that the Human Rights Commission was created by Mister Charlie—after a previous bath of crocodile tears—to help minority races get a better deal from white society. Mister Charlie meant well at the time. At the same time, however, he wrote into the rules that the commission would have absolutely no authority to effect any changes that he might not like. That's also why black folk did not dance in the streets a few days ago when Mister Charlie—dripping crocodile tears all over the floors in both houses of Congress—rushed an open-housing bill to the White House. It was signed into law that black men must be allowed to rent and buy housing wherever they damned well please. We black folks understood: Mister Charlie was at it again. He undoubtedly feels much better after granting that boon. He undoubtedly feels, too, that if black folks try to make him live up to the letter and spirit of his shiny new housing law—well, he can always get a decision in his favor from the Manhattan Supreme Court.

The second news item I referred to was an explanation by the Daughters of the American Revolution—those fierce defenders of American ideals—about why they don't accept black daughters as members. The D.A.R. said most black folks at the time of the Revolution were slaves, and slaves didn't keep the kind of birth records you need to prove kinship with the patriots.

Furthermore, said the D.A.R., if some black lady happens to show up with records that prove her kinship with Crispus Attucks—a black man who was killed by British soldiers in the Boston Massacre of 1770—she is still out of luck. Why? "Because Crispus Attucks was not a Revolutionary. He was a rioter. He actually took part in a riot which was held before the established date of the Revolution, April 19, 1775."

So much for Crispus Attucks. So much for the Boston Massacre, which took place about five years too soon.

Dear Son,

This is another footnote, Adam. I suddenly realized this evening that I had given you almost everybody's view of your daddy, but not my own.

Aside from being a madman, and proud of it, I see myself as a better-than-average human being in the things that really count: compassion, intelligence and talent. And I should add that I make no pretense at modesty.

And how does your compassionate, intelligent, talented and immodest daddy live day by day?

Mostly in the crevices of this society. I have come to prefer it that way because my madness puts me at odds with so many of the institutions, organizations and individuals making up the American landscape.

I have built my life around my family, my search for personal wisdom, a few trusted friends, my work, books, theater and music—in that order. I make a special effort, however, to carry out my share of joint responsibility, whether I have accepted it willingly or have simply found myself honor-bound to it. And after punching dozens of people in the nose as a younger man—especially whites—I have finally learned to walk away.

Although my friends are few, they last. I believe that is because I avoid making commitments I cannot keep; because I try to be honest and fair with them; I listen to them as well as talk to them; I try not to demand anything of them that I would not be willing to do on their behalf, and I resist the temptation to try forcing them into accepting my values. Instead of trying to reform my friends, I concentrate on reforming me; to make myself the best kind of human being I can. That, in my opinion, is everybody's primary job.

I won't pretend that I have done all there is to be done. I still have a long way to go. But I am making progress. As the years go by, for example, I am able to tell fewer and fewer lies. It is possible, of course, that your daddy is off on the wrong track. But I feel in my bones, as a serious student of the best minds in history, that I am right.

If you asked me to sum up the substance of my adult self, I would say that I have tried to be on the level with myself and with the rest of the world; I have tried my best to be a man.

Dear Adam,

In my very first letter, Adam-Smasher, I said that I think there's a way to deal with this society's racial madness, peacefully and effectively, if Mister Charlie is man enough to face it. But, as you realize by now, facing things squarely is not how Mister Charlie made his reputation.

I don't say my answer is easy to face. On the contrary. But I do say it is within human possibility, though at the moment it may seem only the dream of a tortured imagination.

On the life-size television screen in my mind I see Mister Charlie trying bravely to face my answer. Which demands facing the ugly, demented thing that created the black monster he fears: Himself.

The scene is a featureless plain in the middle of nowhere. The sky and the ground, the air itself, seem gray. In the center of the picture on a dull white throne sits the greatest Mister Charlie of them all—well dressed, pink-jowled, benign. He waits patiently to receive the Chief Negotiator for black men.

He broods over the war that has led to this confrontation: Sporadic violence led by an army of H. Rap Browns, spilling barrels of blood in the streets, and a relentless campaign of civil disobedience led by the heirs of Dr. Martin Luther King, disrupting Mister Charlie's business-as-usual in thirty-one major cities—sit-downs, stall-ins, marches, boycotts and blockades by tens of black thousands, far too many to throw into jail.

194

Now there is a truce, and the future—if any—hangs on this meeting. Mister Charlie is prepared and determined.

Then yonder on the gray horizon appears a lone black man in shirt sleeves, slowly advancing with all deliberate speed toward Mister Charlie on the throne. He is the Chief Negotiator. His walk seems familiar. It is then that I recognize him as myself.

"Sorry to have kept you waiting," I say in a voice that is not sorry in the least. "But this assignment came as something of a surprise to me." *That* is true.

"Think nothing of it," he says cheerfully, rising and extending his right hand. His handshake is firm and sincere.

"Well, now," he says, sizing me up with his benign clear blue eyes. "You look to me like a reasonable boy—uh—man. Sorry about that; it's the way I was brought up, I guess."

"I know exactly how you were brought up," I say as evenly as possible for me. "Let's get down to business."

"Agreed, agreed," he says, nodding four times as he sits down again on the throne. "And let me say right off the bat that there is no problem so big that it can't be solved by reasonable men reasoning together. I'm confident that we can lick this thing. To show you what I mean, my people have authorized me to make an offer that I'm sure you will find both useful and attractive. A one-billion-dollar crash program."

He pauses to let it sink in.

"We'll spend it however you want," he adds paternally. "To create more jobs for nigras; to build more housing in nigra communities; to increase their welfare benefits, or we can spread it out over all three. And mind you, this one-billion-dollar crash program is not just for one year. We mean one billion dollars in each of the next five years. All you've got to do now is just tell me where you want the first billion to go."

"Up yours," I say, slowly and distinctly. I feel no anger, only weariness and a deep disgust. Like I'm hearing something I have already heard too many times before.

Mister Charlie turns red from neck to scalp. But he forces a smile and a chuckle. He has come here to negotiate. Pretending to have missed my meaning, he asks, "What would you say if we raised the ante to a couple of billion a year for each of the next five years?"

"Up yours," I tell him again in the same tone. I am vaguely aware that I should perhaps be making a counterproposal at this point. But something tells me to wait, that he will not be able to hear me, really, until he has pulled all his sorry wares from that carpetbag he calls a heart.

I can see him swallowing his anger once again. He is not a quitter.

"Suppose we table that matter for the moment," he says patiently, "and come back to it a bit later. I probably should have started with what I'm about to give you now: an unmistakable sign of our good faith. We are prepared to pass a Civil Rights Act giving nigras the right to marry whites, if both parties in the marriage submit first to a painless sterilization process to prevent any children. I'm sure you can appreciate that without the sterilization the thought of our race being blacked out, so to speak, would haunt us."

Great ghosts in the graveyard! Is that what they've been afraid of all these years?

I am still not angry, just exasperated. Enough to pinch what seems to be his most exposed and sensitive nerve.

196

"Mister Charlie," I say, "will you never learn? Black-and-white marriage is not what this is all about. The only thing we want you to do about mixed marriage is to stop pretending that the rules against it don't serve to curb some white appetites as well as black ones. You talked just now of giving blacks the right to marry whites, for example. As if the white partners in mixed marriages were somehow not involved. Do you know of any cases where blacks have proposed to whites at the point of a pistol? Or marched the whites at gunpoint to doctors' offices to get blood tests; then to the marriage bureaus to get licenses, and then down the aisle of churches to say 'I do' against their will?"

Mister Charlie is indignant.

"I never said there weren't some foolish, misguided whites in our society," he says. "But you can't judge us all by the foolish actions of a few. That's not fair."

I count to ten very slowly. After all, I also have come to negotiate.

After a deep, deep breath, I say calmly, "You don't know it, Mister Charlie, but in a way you have just defined the problem we came here to solve. The problem of recognizing what is fair for both of us at the same time. Can't you see that you are again using one standard of fair play for whites and another for blacks? And can't you see that your double standard is the stuff that riots and revolutions are made of?

"If you can't see that, we might as well call off these negotiations right now as a waste of time; because all proposals to solve the problem hinge on recognizing what the problem is. So I think maybe we should recess this meeting to let you sleep on that. We can try again tomorrow.

"But before I go, let me leave you with a P.S. about

mixed marriage. As far as we're concerned, you can pass a Federal law that absolutely forbids it under any circumstances. That would work both ways, you know; protecting our blackness as much as it guarded your mania for whiteness."

Mister Charlie is flabbergasted, disbelief written in his eyes. "Are you trying to tell me," he says, "that nigras *like* being black?"

"Of course we like it," I say matter-of-factly. "Black is what we are. And we don't see it as being worse than any other color. Can you imagine a tiger not liking his stripes?"

"Then why," he asks, "do nigras spend millions of dollars every year trying to change their skins to look white?"

"For the same reason," I tell him, "that white soldiers paint their faces black in the darkness: To make themselves less conspicuous targets in a hostile country. Good day, sir."

A light rain is falling when next we meet on the same gray plain out yonder. The rain, too, seems gray.

Mister Charlie, back on his throne, is protected by a dull white canopy. I stand before him, once again in shirt sleeves, holding a black umbrella.

"Let's hope we can do good work here today," he says hopefully.

"That depends," I say flatly, "on whether you took a long, hard look at yourself last night."

"I did that," he assures me, nodding energetically. "I most certainly did."

"What did you see?"

Mister Charlie pauses a moment to pick over his

thoughts and words. He senses that this is a critical stage in the negotiations, and he does not want to blow it. Then, focusing his serene blue eyes on the middle distance, he says, "I saw a man who has made mistakes. Blunders really. But I also saw a man who is willing to correct those blunders. To be fair."

"And how do you propose to go about being fair?" I ask.

He shifts his gaze from the middle distance and peers directly into my eyes. What an actor! Then in a voice dripping humility he says:

"Well, to be honest, I'll need your help on that. But I know we must have peace. And I'm prepared to commit my people to giving you people anything that's reasonable to help you."

"Take a deep breath, Mister Charlie," I say. "And brace yourself."

"I'm ready," he says, leaning forward on his throne.

"Well, to begin with," I say, "we don't want you to give us anything. In fact, we want you to stop giving us things. To stop creating jobs for blacks. To stop building houses for blacks. To stop passing civil rights laws for blacks. To stop all of your crash programs for blacks."

Having handed him that large, hard rock, I pause to let him digest it.

Mister Charlie blinks. "You don't want any of those things?" he asks slowly. "Better jobs, better housing, better education and so forth?"

"On the contrary," I say. "We want them all. But not on those miserable terms. We are perfectly willing to take our chances with everybody else in this society in pursuit of those goals. We insist, however, on having the same chance as everybody else to reach those goals on our own."

Seeing his puzzled expression, I pause again. Mister Charlie is not getting the message.

"Look at it this way," I say patiently. "Suppose for a moment that our society is a football game, the blacks against the whites. Well, the way the rules are now, every time the blacks get the ball the situation automatically becomes fourth down and eighty-nine yards to go. Not an impossible situation, but damn near it. No chance to make a steady, well-planned advance by our own strength and ingenuity."

A faint flicker of comprehension lights Mister Charlie's blue eyes. "I can see that that wouldn't be fair in football," he says, "but I don't think it's like that in our society. Our laws forbid that kind of unfairness. Of course, there are some of my people who hate nigras. But surely you understand that we can't pass a law to make people love one another."

Once again, I count to ten very slowly.

Then I say, "Love has nothing to do with it. You can believe that we don't find you lovable. I'm talking about fair play. You can like or dislike whoever you damn well please. What we want you to see is that even though you also dislike white murderers, white rapists, white Communists and white traitors, you are extremely careful not to deny them the basic human right of fair treatment under the law. You even set them free—despite their confessions —if they can prove that you denied them that right, by accident or design."

Mister Charlie raises a hand to interrupt me. "I think you will have to admit that you are overstating the case," he says politely. "Except for a few isolated pockets of prejudice, such as Mississippi, our courts—"

"That's a lie," I say hotly. "And besides, I was not referring to the courts alone. That was just a handy, obvious example. The truth is your whole society is unfair except for isolated pockets of enlightenment. If you can't admit that, you can never solve the problem; because the only way to do it is to stop giving first aid to your mutilated victims and start cracking down hard on the mutilators."

There is a long gray silence as we fix each other with angry eyes in the rain.

Finally, Mister Charlie slumps back on his throne and sighs. "I don't see how in the world—" he begins.

"I'll tell you how," I say. Then, seeing that he accepts my interruption, I continue as calmly as possible for me. "Basically, it means that black men must no longer be denied the right to live where they choose, if they can pay the going price. And blacks must have equal access to the price. Which means that labor unions—like those in the construction industry—can no longer be allowed to bar black men from membership, or admit them on some quota. That is the only way to brake the cycle of poverty that traps each black generation in its turn. To let black men do it themselves with their own sweat.

"It also means that white employers can no longer be allowed to reject black applicants who are qualified for the jobs that are open, especially jobs above the menial level that pay something higher than a bare living wage. Neither can the white corporations be allowed to continue denying blacks the same chances for advancement into the upper echelons of the power structure.

"To guarantee black men that much fair play would not

lift us up to your level overnight. But we could lift ourselves that high in a couple of generations. And in the
meantime there would be peace because there was justice
and hope."

I pause again for Mister Charlie's benefit. He has another hard rock to digest. And harder ones still to come.

"I suppose now," he says wearily, "you're going to tell
me that guaranteeing all those things is possible."

"Certainly," I say. "All it takes is guts. You could
begin by establishing a Federal Set-Things-Right Commission in every town and community to bypass and over-
ride the existing instruments of oppression. You could
finance those commissions with those billions you are so
anxious to spend on crash programs for blacks. Staff those
commissions with blacks, whites and in-betweens. And give
them the authority to correct wrongs and set things right on
the spot. Instead of letting the wrong continue while the
complaint is dragged from court to court over the years.

"If a black man or any other man calls the commission,
for example, and says he has been denied a job or membership in a union for some stupid reason such as his race
or religion, the commission sends a team to the spot. Then.
Not next month. The first thing the commission team does
is to shut down the company or whatever construction project the union is involved in. And keep it shut until the
complaint has been settled. That means the company's
offices are evacuated. Electricity, water and mail deliveries
and pickups are cut off.

"That will guarantee cooperation for speedy investiga-
tion of the complaint. Instead of double talk among lawyers. It is a simple matter to determine whether a black
man is capable and qualified for a particular job. You don't

need lawyers for that. It is also a simple matter to determine whether the company has indicated that it needs a man of his qualifications. By advertising, for example.

"If the commission team finds that he is not qualified, or that the company has not been seeking a man of his talents in the first place, he is heavily fined for having filed a false complaint. But if his complaint is valid, the commission team lets the company know that it will never be allowed to resume its operations until that black man is accepted as a bona fide part of the company. The same for a union or a factory or other places of business.

"In a case involving fair housing, the entire building would be evacuated from top to bottom, and locked by the Set-Things-Right Commission. If necessary, the commission team could call in Federal troops to see that the building remains sealed. Until the complaint has been settled.

"We realize that such a procedure would adversely affect many whites on the sidelines who could say that they were not responsible. But fair play is everybody's responsibility in this society. It's what America is supposed to be about, in fact. And we believe that it would take only a few crackdowns like that in each community to bury the notions in so many white minds that they can get away with being unfair to blacks, or that unfairness on the part of other whites is no concern of theirs. Instead, because of the crackdowns, even those silent, uninvolved whites would see the necessity for joining an informal society for the prevention of injustice, so that every man, black or otherwise, is treated fairly.

"There may be less drastic ways to force those whites who behave like hunkies to obey the basic law, but we don't believe so. If there is a better way, you can only find it by

committing as much of your energy and resources to po-
licing hunkies as you have committed to investigating their
victims and organizing first-aid projects designed to relieve
their symptoms, but not their basic complaint."

Mister Charlie pulls out a notebook and a ballpoint pen.
"Let me get some of this down on paper," he says. "Now
as I understand it, you want us to crack down hard on
bigots; make labor unions, employers and landlords treat
nigras like they treat whites. Under the threat of having
their places shut down by a Federal Set-Things-Right
Commission. Or Federal troops if necessary."

"Precisely," I say.

He begins writing, then stops in mid-sentence. Looking
at me suspiciously, he says: "These are some pretty strange
ideas. Have you people been listening by any chance to
those Communist agitators?"

I explode. "Do blacks need reds to show them how dirty
whites can be?"

He ducks his head and goes back to writing in his notebook. "I just meant that this is very radical stuff you people are demanding," he says apologetically. "Downright
un-American."

"We are not concerned with labels," I tell him calmly.
"Only with justice. And now that you've got that written
down, let's get on to the next point."

He looks up in open-mouthed surprise. "You mean there
is something else besides this stuff?" He practically shouts
it.

"Yes," I say, smiling for the very first time. "Just one
more thing. In a way, the most important thing of all. You
may have noticed that I've said nothing about schools or
education. That's because we feel that school integration

would come as a matter of unavoidable fact. Like the falling rain. If the basic demands are met on job opportunities, fair housing and equal protection under the law. In other words, there is nothing wrong with the neighborhood school system—letting kids go to school in the neighborhood they live in—if the neighborhood is not closed to blacks because they are black or because they are systematically denied the chance to make the kind of money it takes for anyone to live there.

"Now we come to what I said a moment ago was the most important thing of all: Our proposal concerning the educational process itself. As you have it set up now, it fails to warn the children forthrightly that their society is in danger of destroying itself; and that it will almost certainly succeed unless they and future generations repair the damage by rejecting the stupidities of the past.

"They must be shown exactly what these glaring stupidities are, in a regular course of instruction. Like geography and arithmetic. A course that might be called American Hypocrisy."

Mr. Charlie splutters, but does not interrupt. I go on.

"The textbook could be a daily newspaper; and most of the field research could be done by occasional exposures to the classroom television set. Let them see and tell them what they are seeing; and why it is a menace to their society. Let them know that decay is inevitable in any community of men as long as there is a wide gap between the things they say and the things they do day by day.

"Show them, for example, the laws and court decisions that this society has used to deny its commitment to fair play, and to justify its treatment of black men as lesser forms of human life.

"Show them specific cases in which a law is enforced one way against the rich, another way against the poor.

"Help them to understand how and why the deprived classes are constantly advised to be patient and peaceful, and what forces are driving them toward rebellion.

"Help them to recognize the dishonest claims that corporations are allowed to present in advertisements and commercials in the name of free enterprise and competition."

This time, Mister Charlie can't restrain himself.

"Now, just a minute," he says. "Aren't you getting a little bit out of your depth? Telling us what to do about you is one thing. What to do about our own business is something very different."

"Lying to blacks or lying to whites is still lying," I reply, surprised by my own calm. "If it weren't for the lies that twist your society, I wouldn't be standing out here in this damned rain.

"To get back to your own business, why don't you try showing them the small headlines buried on page thirty-nine of the daily newspaper about price-fixing by rival corporations to avoid competition as much as possible; and the light slaps on the wrist the offenders receive when caught, in contrast with their heavy profits during the lengthy conspiracy.

"Tell them what a lie is, and give them specific examples from the daily mouthings of politicians."

"I hate to keep interrupting," he interrupts. "But you can't possibly mean to say that politicians are liars. Not only are most of them good, decent, honest men, but many of them have been mighty white to you people." He winks.

"Mister Charlie," I say, feeling like a horse with a fly buzzing around his head, "do you remember what Jesse Owens, a black runner who burned Herr Charlie's ass with an Olympic torch, said about newspapers? He said that a black man believes less and less of them as he reads his way to the front from the sports pages. And those front pages are filled with what politicians say.

"You might point out, for instance, in this course on American Hypocrisy, that while this country's leading statesmen make speech after speech about halting the armaments race among nations, it is this country that sells more armaments overseas than any other country in the world, year after year after year.

"Explain to them," I go on, getting back into the swing of it, "how merchants consistently cheat their customers by giving them less than they bargain for and charging them more than what is fair. And how the customers cheat the merchants by simply taking what they need and not paying anything at all."

"That sounds like looting," Mister Charlie breaks in again, without even raising his face from his notebook. "But you'd know more about that than I do."

"Not half as much as you could teach us. You might tell them, for example, what bribes and kickbacks are. That's on a much bigger scale. Show them the long list of documented cases, to alert them to the commonness and variety of situations where illegal payoffs breed and flourish."

"Okay, okay," he says. "I hope that's all of it now."

"Not quite," I answer, drawing a deep breath.

"Explain to them that most of those tragically comic human cartoons called hippies, beatniks and dropouts are

207

part of a growing clan of independent thinkers who have recognized the pervasive corruption in their society, and have rejected it.

"Explain to them also that their society is but a larger version of the families they live with in their homes; that if the members of a family consistently lie to one another, cheat one another, steal from one another and treat one another unjustly, the family becomes an angry hostile thing divided against itself, torn by ever-increasing hate and mounting violence.

"And make it clear to them that the corruption, the hate and the violence will only get worse as long as they accept, as common American practice, the lies and injustices that have brought this society to the brink; that in time they may have to revise or overhaul most of the basic institutions of their society—social, economic and political. And, finally, that the only way that they can have a better world is to become themselves much better as individual human beings."

Mister Charlie is writing furiously, head down. I stand quietly in the soft gray rain, exhausted and less than optimistic.

At last he says: "Phew! What a workout! When you get wound up, you really go." He smiles and closes his notebook.

"Now about these proposals," he says, abruptly changing to a serious mood. "We didn't expect anything at all like this. I'm not saying we won't consider them. On their merits. But I'll have to take them back to my people so they can study them for the next few months. That may sound like I'm trying to put you off, but I'm not. It's a question of discussing these things among ourselves like reasonable men, the way we always do, and then putting it to a vote.

"After all, boy," he says with a broad, friendly smile, "this *is* a democracy, you know. Heh, heh, heh."

Dear Adam my son,

Here's the final letter
that your mad immodest daddy
leaves for you
I am filled with doubts and fears
that I haven't told you things
that a saner sort of daddy
really ought to

I have tried to give you insights
on this world, myself, our race
warned you to be on guard
lest they hold you down in place
But have I filled your mind with hate
and failed to show a trace
of the love and hope your daddy has
for the hapless human race

Have I shown you how to laugh
how to face the things you fear
Have I said it's not unmanly
for a man to shed a tear
And have I told you also
that the world has nonwhite joy
that there are even miracles
like the smile of a brown-skinned boy

Have I said you owe me nothing
that my love, my gifts are free
that all I ask of you, my son,

is that you simply be
Have I left the clues to guide you
through the maze that is your life
Have I indicated why you'll need
a cause, a friend, a wife

Have I hinted at surprises
neither black nor white but gray
like the fact that life is empty
if you spend it all at play
like the satisfactions found in work
in sacrifice and giving
like the meanings found in love and art
that change still life to living

Have I shown that you can reach the sky
if you believe you can
Have I helped you toward the courage
to stand up and be a man
And have I made it obvious
in anecdote or rhyme
that what I wish for all black men
is freedom in your time